The Thangs Mama Nem Said

Earl Mills

Foreword By: Doro Bush Koch

Published By:
Jasher Press & Co.
www.jasherpress.com
customerservice@jasherpress.com
1.888.220.2068
P.O. Box 14520
New Bern, NC 28561

ISBN: **978-0692548936**

First Edition
Printed and bound in the United States of America

The Thangs Mama Nem

Earl Mills
Foreword By: Doro Bush Koch

Said

FOREWORD

The great African-American civil rights activist Frederick Douglass said, "Once you learn to read, you will be forever free." What a valuable lesson for all of us and especially for the author Earl Mills, who at 48 years, learned to read and then published several books, sharing his love of family, poetry, and literacy. Learning to read changed his life.

My mom and former First Lady Barbara Bush understood early on that helping individuals learn to read can make an enormous difference in one's life. And Earl Mills is a living example. As Mills witnessed, literacy programs can become a lifeline for so many adults with low-literacy skills. His commitment to improving his literacy skills helped him to live out his dream of becoming a poet and author. My mom would be so proud of him, and we are honored to recognize your achievements.

Every day more than 36 million adult Americans are reading at or below a third-grade level, struggling to obtain jobs, to help their child with homework, or simply to read a prescription bottle. Yet, Earl is such an inspirational story for all of us – a story of hope and courage where he overcame his fears to strive for a better self. More importantly, Earl realized that learning to read liberated him.

Literacy unlocked his creative potential and God-given talents. With the right tools and resources, Mills made the bold decision to improve his life and devote his time to encouraging others to learn to read. Bold, brave and inspirational are three words that best describe Mills as he traveled many roads to find his way.

For black slaves, access to books or learning to read was incredibly difficult. They learned through stories and songs told and sung by their mothers, fathers, or grandparents. Many of these stories were passed on from generation to generation. Earl Mills masterfully captures and recreates the songs and tales of African Americans who share their sadness, hardship and courage during a time when slaves could only think of daily toil and survival. These stories, poems and songs have shaped a culture that is embedded in American history.

Today, as we still see communities facing poverty, racial tensions, and inequality, Mills offers us hope. He reminds us that we must always remember the struggles and passions of the slaves in our country who did not experience freedom for a long time, yet carried the torch of hope that one day they would be free.

Earl Mills has achieved the American dream and now can express his love of reading through his beautiful words that inspire us all. May we continue to see more of Earl Mills' fine works as he is a reminder to all of us that literacy can help individuals and families improve their lives.

Doro Bush Koch, Honorary Chairman of The Barbara Bush Foundation for Family Literacy
July 2015

ENDORSEMENT

When Earl asked me to write the foreword to this book, I saw in my mind's eye, the third grader who sat in the back of his classroom; bullied and intimidated by the printed word. He was like millions of other innocent children who were sent off to school with high hopes of learning how to read.

He was promoted to the 3rd, 4th, and 5th grades; he graduated from high school reading at or below elementary level. Not knowing how to read has a demoralizing impact on the individual and our great nation. I love the quote from the book, *A Tree Grows in Brooklyn* –"Oh, magic hour when a child first knows she(he) can read printed words."

Oh how long Earl Mills wait for the magic hour when he could finally read the printed word and read his first book at the age of forty-eight. What Earl should have, could have, learned at 8, he learned at 48. This tells us that it is never too late to learn how to read and write. No matter how smart or clever a person may be in America today, no individual can maximize his or her fullest potential without developing basic literacy skills. The first three years of our formal education we learn to read and for the rest of our lives, we read to learn.

The joy of conquering a lifelong struggle in adulthood has motivated and encouraged Earl to write stories and poetry of his life experiences, including his difficult journey to literacy. Earl has offered us hope, given us joy and provided us with a better understanding of the struggle that millions of children, teens, and adults face today. Thank you, Earl, for your honesty and creativity. Thank you to the reader, for reading Earl's stories and realizing the strength and vulnerability it takes to expose one's own story. **Write on Earl, write on.**

Learning how to read has filled a big hole in Earl's soul and teaching all of our children, teens, and adults how to read will help fill a big hole in America's soul. Teaching a person how to read is an act of love. As slave abolitionist, Frederick Douglass wrote, "Once you learn to read, you will be forever free."

John Corcoran

National literacy advocate and author of *The Teacher who couldn't Read* and *The Bridge to Literacy*

INTRODUCTION

Writing this book was a challenge; I laughingly joke around and say that this was like writing a real book. My first three books were poetry which is what I believe to be my God given gift. My last assessment about five years ago at Craven Literacy Council in New Bern, North Carolina was at a ninth and a half or tenth grade reading level and my spelling has been an uphill climb. So if you need a partner in a spelling bee, I probably shouldn't be your first choice. Never the less during this process I found myself having to depend on others to complete this book which brought back a lot of unpleasant memories. My first goal for finishing this book was August or September of 2014 which I missed. My new goal was March of 2015. Which I missed, It is now late May, and I am sweating anxiously with anticipation to meet my new goal May, 2015. But in spite of all the set-backs this book has also been a lot of fun, and I have enjoyed gathering all of the funny and meaningful things of the past and reminiscing on them.

The people I work with at Hatteras Yachts, attend church with at Dayspring Ministry, my family and my friends are all country. They usually talk country without even knowing it, so when I first started writing I learned to have a pen and paper with me at all times in order to catch memorable moments. It is not uncommon for me to gather eight or ten things a day. Now the people I work with and my church family will come up to me and say "I have one for your book." There are too many names to mention so I just want to say thank you to everyone who helped make this book possible. And as you read this book you can say "I gave Earl that one."

I DEDICATE THIS BOOK TO MY THIRTEEN SIBLINGS

I dedicate this book to my thirteen siblings Lenora Mills, Leroy Mills, Roger Howard, Curtis Raye Staten, Zebbie King-memborn, Arletha Staten-Dunk, Marilyn Staten-Lawson, Sheila Staten, Joyce Staten-Ingram, Veronica Staten-Baker, Ylonda Staten, Seth Staten, Lora Staten, and Cynthia Staten-Mitchell. We lost Curtis Raye Staten, Lenora Mills, and Leroy Mills, Curtis was premature weighing only two pounds and five ounces. He lived only five days from July eighteenth to July the twenty third nineteen fifty four. He was buried in a shoe box. Lenora Mills lost her fight with cancer on February- twenty first, two thousand and six. We lost our oldest brother Leroy better known as "High Boot" on March ninth two thousand and fifteen one year to the day that we all got together for the cover shot for this book.

One of the old saying is that a big family is and happy family, I have found this to be true. I cherish all of our memories happy and sad, for the laughter we've shared, the times we've cried together, and the challenges that we've faced and overcame. I believe that this has forged in us the true sense of family, a family that has always encouraged and supported each other, a family that I am proud to say that I am a part of.

MY FIRST THOUGHTS ABOUT THIS BOOK

The Thangs Mama'nem Said

My first thoughts about this book "The Thangs Mama' nem Said, was around 2008. After reading one of Langston Hughes's poems in the dialog of African Americans after slavery, the broken English, and what I like to call the laze tongued poem, awakened something within me and inspired me to try and write one of my own, that birthed the poem "Devil Keep On Bother'n Me." This caused me to think about the sayings I heard my great grandparents, grandparents, parents and the older people in my community use, and caused me to realize that this dialog and the sayings were slowly fading away. This made me realize that my children and grandchildren had never heard most of these sayings. In no way am I implying that we should teach our children to speak this way. I am a firm believer in using correct grammar, and speaking correctly. This book is just one way of taking a peak into our past, preserving it for the future and maybe in the process we just might get one of them gut busting laughs on the way.

REFLECTING A TIME WHEN LIFE WAS SIMPLE

This book reflects a time when life was simple. When a man's word was his bond, when men looked each other dead in the eyes with a firm hand shake and it was a binding contact. When children were seen and not heard. When you knew your neighbor and your neighbor was your friend. When men earned a living by the sweat of their brow and took pride in a hard day's work. When yes sir, and no sir, was always used by young people. Children would spend their weekends and summers outside playing games and making things like homemade slingshots, bow in arrows, and pop guns, they would catch tadpoles in the ditches. Not spending time in the house on the computer. Down in the southern part of North Carolina, we might not dot every i or cross every t, in our back woods way of talking. But when I look back with fond memories, I realize that that simple times in life was not so bad after all.

Earl Mills the son of an illiterate sharecropper, brother to thirteen siblings, father of five children, has hailed the same job for forty two years, read over one hundred books, wrote over one hundred and fifty poems, authored five books, shared the stage with formal First Lady Mrs. Barbara Bush, and at the age of forty five he walked into Craven literacy Council in New Bern, North Carolina, and was assessed at a second grade reading level, because when he graduated from high school in 1971 he could not read.

This is his fifth book "The Thangs Mama'Nam Said", this is out-of-the-box for Earl, his first four books, "From

Illiterate To Poet" "From Illiterate To Author" "The Poet Who Could Not Read" and "The Illiterate Poet trilogy" Were poetry Earl's normal line of writing. So this was quite a challenge and at the same time fun.

I have mentioned before that my spelling has been an uphill climb, and I have not yet reached the top. So I had to reach out for help to finish this book. And I was fortunate enough to find it. In Kamesia Dixon, Orianna Best, Sherry Rodgers, and Etta Marie Mills; which I made dictations too. My wife Marie is what I call my sounding board when I have trouble spelling a word I would bounce them off of her, so thanks for all of your help, and I am still climbing, the top is within reach.

NUGGETS OF WISDOM

When we were growing up our parents were sharecroppers then we lived in other people houses and helped them on the farm. So we moved a lot, one day we were moving and mom had us cleaning the house, inside and outside even under the house. So I asked mom, why are we cleaning this house it was dirty when we moved here. And she replied, it might have been dirty when we moved here. But I will not let anyone say that we left a house dirty. Because I do not want to be known as someone that is dirty. This is just one of many life-changing things that Mama them used to say. Things to live by, things that would build character, and shape lives.

One day we were in the yard with mama and the people that own the house that we live in and help on the farm came up. With things to give to mom, she took them and said thank you, when they left I asked mama, why did you take those things we don't need them. And she replied, we might not need these things, but if we say no, one day they will have something that we need, and they won't give it to us. As a young man I experienced this in my life. One Sunday a prominent person in the community knocked on my door knowing that we had a lot of children and offered me some furniture I said no, and that was the last time he ever offered me anything. So the things that Mama and them said were not just sayings, they were wisdom to live by. I should have listened, I learned later the furniture were antiques.

I feel fortunate to have had so many people in my life with nuggets of wisdom. One of them was my great uncle Bert Mills from Trenton North Carolina. He was always talking to us young folks of the ripe old age of about nine and ten years old. This particular afternoon he was talking to us and said. If you had two men one who made $100 and the other making $50, if the man that made $50 a week saved five dollars and the man that made $100 did not save anything, the man that made $50 would be better off. I always wondered why uncle Bert spent his time talking to young boys in this manner, now I realize that it was just the thing that Mama and them used to say. I think that there should be more of this going on today shaping the lives of our young people and just maybe there would not be as much violence in the world today.

One of my jobs after graduating high school was working at a little mint in Kinston North Carolina the work was okay, but the pay was not. I was thinking about getting married and this little bit of money was not going to cut it. So I told my father that I was going to quit. I told him how much money I made and he agreed that it was not much money. Then he said something that I have never forgot, he said that is not much money, but if I were you I would stay until I found another job. I was what I thought to be a grown man, so I did not have to do it, but I did, that nugget of wisdom has served me well since graduating high school. There has only been two weeks in my life that I have not had a job so I am so thankful for all the things that Mama them said.

Who's gonna (going to) fix massa's (master's) breakfast?

One Sunday morning about five years ago, I was at my church Dayspring ministries in New Bern, NC. Pastor P.O. Rodgers was ministering and in his message he used an illustration. It was a family story that had been passed down through the generations about how his family was gathered with the other slaves to be told by the master of the end of slavery. After the announcement, Pastor's great great great aunt Eliza said to a family member: "Who's gonna fix massa's breakfast?" I began to think of how the shackles didn't just bind the slave's hands and feet, but it also shackled their minds and how the remnants seemed to linger on. So I wrote down the saying "who's gonna fix massa's breakfast", not knowing when or where I would use it. I think I have found a suitable place in this book.

JONATHAN RODGERS

My name is Jonathan E. R. Okon and I was born and raised in Batimore, MD. But the homestead of my mother's family is Craven County, North Carolina; the cities of New Bern and Havelock to be exact. I first got into genealogy at the young age of 13, a month before my 14th birthday and one month before the start of my high school tenure; A rare time to get involved since most get into genealogical research much later in the twilight of their lives. My mother's family usually have their reunion every two years falling on the even years. It was my grandmother, Mary Fenner Rodgers, who got me started into genealogy, at least indirectly. It was the Summer of '98 and she handed me the reunion pamphlet from the '94 Reunion. It had everything in it; it had almost every name, every ancestor, and date. The sight of it nearly knocked me off my feet. To have your whole history at the palms of your hands was mind-blowing. I had so many questions for my grandmother and her two sisters, my great-aunts, Carlillie Fenner Hill and Rosa Lee Fenner Bell. "Who's this?, Who's that?" And the story I shared is one of many that came from them...

J. E. R. OKON

My 3rd great grandmother, Eliza Jane Phillips-Farrior, was born a slave in Duplin County, NC around the year of 1834. Her father's name was John Waters (or Walters) with her mother's name being unknown. She met and married John Nick Becton on December 24, 1851 in Carteret County, NC, but couldn't make it official until August of 1866 because slaves couldn't officially get married. Between the two, they had 8 children; five boys and three girls. Eliza was a cook for the master in the big house. One of few prominent positions and stature amongst slaves. And she was a great cook from what I've heard in family stories. That's why there are so many great cooks in my family.

I imagine Eliza's "gift" had been passed down through the generations. When Eliza was well into adulthood, the Civil War had started, 1860 to be exact, and the slaves were soon abolished by President Lincoln in 1863 making slavery unconstitutional by the laws of the Emancipation Proclamation. As Eliza and the rest of the slaves were

21

gathered to be told the news by the master, she pondered to herself about the big announcement. She said to a family member, "whose gonna cook masta's food now?" Someone repied, "You don't have to, youse free now!!!...."

Steven K. Bell, Attorney at Law

I first met Mr. Steven Bell around 1998, when my wife Marie and I were closing on our new home. We remember it as a professional and pleasant experience. Over the years in several real estate matters, we have found this to still be true. When looking for a location that would complement the time period of this book, I remembered the historic house with large white chairs on the front porch that serves as Mr. Bell's law office.

I want to thank Mr. Bell for the use of his office for the cover shot of "The Thang Mama Nem Said." In practice since 1994, Mr. Bell is an experienced attorney. Mr. Bell is a lifelong resident of New Bern, so he knows this area well. While he primarily handles residential real estate closings, he also prepares wills, handles estates, represents corporations, and offers advice to small businesses.

For Steven Bell and his committed staff, you come first. You'll receive the time and attention that a hometown office can dedicate to seeing that your needs are met. Your legal matters will be handled confidentially, ethically and with attention to the smallest detail.

Steven K. Bell
Attorney at Law
(252)633-1236 ext. 25
(252) 633-1524 (fax)
506 Pollock Street
New Bern, NC 28562

THANKS TO A CO-WORKER

I want to thank Erin Riddick a co-worker, we worked together for about a year. We had a lot in common. We worked, laughed, and talked. I don't know how or when we started talking about the old sayings from the past. But what else would two old country boys talk about. One day I started writing some of them down, and before I knew it they started to add up, not knowing at the time that those sayings on paper towels, torn paper bags, and scrap pieces of paper would become my fifth book. Erin has been one of my biggest encouragers from the beginning of this book. So once again I say thanks.

MY FRIEND EARL

I first met Earl Mills in 1982, while working for Hatteras Yachts. Earl had transferred from the main production plant to the launch and make ready area, where I worked as the electrical quality assurance inspector. I found Earl to be a friendly, outgoing individual with a great sense of humor.

Sometime later Earl was out in charge of working off the punch-list of items that I would find during my inspections. Quite often, Earl would have a helper or two, and they would work off the checklist as a team. I think Earl would say to his helper, "you have the checklist, read that next item off to me". On the occasions when Earl was working by himself, he would frequently come to me, checklist in hand, and say, "what do you mean by this item here". Without a clue as to why Earl needed explanation, I would describe what I was looking for, and Earl would go perform the task without fail. Sometimes, he would even include two items in his question. Looking back on that now, I realize that Earl must have a pretty good memory.

The term "pretty good" reminds me of another story. Working together as closely as we did, Earl and I became good friends. Each morning, when I would greet Earl, he would respond with the same answer-"pretty good". After a while, I started calling Earl by the name Pretty Good, a nickname which has stuck till this day.

One day, while working together on a boat, Earl came to me and said, "Alden, I have a secret to tell you". Having no idea how serious Earls secret was, I said something like, "what's on your mind buddy?" Without skipping a beat, Earl said, "I can't read". "What? I said in surprise. Holding the checklist in his hand, Earl said again, "I can't read this or anything else for that matter". "I can pick out certain words from memory" Earl said, "but to just pick up a book, or document and start reading, I can't do it. Earl went on to explain how he had gotten to this point, and some of the obstacles and challenges he had faced. At this point, Earl had already taken steps to overcome his handicap. Earl told me that he was enrolled in a reading class through the Craven Literacy Council.

Earl totally shocked me that day, because I had no idea that he could not read. I left Earl with a word of encouragement as we parted. I knew, after having worked with Earl for years and seeing what he was capable of, that Earl would someday realize his dream of being able to read and write. I am proud to know Earl Mills, and I look forward to reading his fifth book sometime very soon.

Alden Harris

DEVIL KEEP ON BOTHERN ME

Dat dare devil keep on bother'n me…
Done told 'em ta gwone.

Don't do dem thangs no mo,
Done went and got myself rebone.

Gwanna go to chuch dis here sundee.
Gwanna praze 'Em all day long.

Devil ain't my massa no mo.
Done told 'em ta gwone.

THE BACK DOOR

No word had to be spoken.
Its message was crystal clear.
Generation after generation.
Would have to enter here.

The back door was so hard to open.
For it held the belittlement of my
kind.
It shackled our will, our souls and our
minds.

The back door was designed.
Engineered and put in place.
It's purpose was to dishonor,
belittle and disgrace.
So that we would never
forget our place.

In silence, it spoke loudly,
It's message still rings today.
Although the front door is available,
Lingering memories seem to stay.

My father entered that door; in shame!
Holding my hand.
I searched my heart, mind and soul.
I did not understand.

The hurt painted a picture
On my father's face.
Will it ever be erased?

As we stand here now.
With faded memories.
Will we ever forget?
Have the seeds that they planted
Fully matured "YET"?

She Toils For Others

Dawn, not yet!
the unoiled hinge squeaks
echoing through a silhouette
of light of Mother's shadow
cast upon her children's faces.

Just another day, like all the rest
she lives to toil for others
leaving her own
to survive for themselves.

As her hand turns the knob
of the back door
her only bestowed entrance
the cascade of light scintillating
through windows not yet cleaned
shows the pain in the hands
that changes the diapers
of children not of her loins.

On tender knees
from midnight prayer
she cleans scuff marks
off shoes that care not
With water stained hand
She cleaned food from fine china
That she owned only when she allowed
Herself to dream.

As the sun touches the tree tops
tender hands turn the knob of the front door
the not yet oiled hinge squeaks.

A smile replaces
the painted one worn all day
now, another day's work ahead
not of toil for it is her own.

I KNOW WHERE I'M SUPPOSED TO SIT

I'm only five, but I know where I'm supposed to sit.
I want to ride, but there is no back seat.
All the other kids are having fun, which seat do I sit upon?
I want to ride the merry-go-round there's no seat for me today.
So I pray
For the day
When it is no longer
This way.

A HOME MADE SLINGSHOT

I rose early that Saturday morning,
Didn't sleep at all that night.
For I already had the perfect,
Forked branch in sight.

With an ax that should been chopping wood,
for the long winter nights.
I skillfully cut the forked,
branch with delight.

I used the tongue from worn out,
Hand-me-down shoes.
I cut out with scissors,
that grandmamma no longer used.

From bicycle tubes,
that could no longer be patched.
I cut strips with the scissors,
which to the forked branch I would attach.

What makes this slingshot special,
is that it wasn't for me.
It's for my little brother,
so I gently wrapped and placed it,
beneath our Christmas Tree.

MY ALMOST NEW CHRISTMAS BIKE

He found a chain sand and oiled it a bit
With tender loving care he made it fit.

He straightened the rim a tube
he'd have to patch
A fender here and there he
would try to match.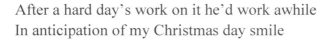

After a hard day's work on it he'd work awhile
In anticipation of my Christmas day smile

I can't remember what my seven-
other siblings got for Christmas that year.
But when I think about that bike-
to my eyes it brings a tear.

For a man that worked too hard-
for the few dollars that he received.
Could not have known the impression-
an almost new bike would leave.

Chrome and spray painted parts sparkled and shine
It wasn't new but I didn't mind.

Craven Literacy Council

Inspiring, hardworking, intelligent, thankful - these are just a few of the words that describe the individuals you will find at Craven Literacy Council (CLC). CLC has been working to improve literacy by providing free, individualized instructional services to residents of Craven, Jones, and Pamlico counties since 1986. CLC accomplishes this mission by using volunteer tutors who are extensively trained by CLC's certified training team in proven techniques for teaching adult learners. CLC offers instruction in the four literacy skills of listening, speaking, reading, and writing along with essential life skills such as reading medication instructions, reading street signs, calling 911, reading a paycheck, calculating money, math skills, computer skills, and communicating with school teachers. With the help of CLC instruction, students become more self-sufficient and strive to reach their personal goals. We are honored to serve individuals like Earl Mills and proud of the difference we are making in the lives of our learners. Literacy touches every area of our student's life and we are thankful for the opportunity to assist individuals who are "Learning for Life".

Donna Marshall
Executive Director
Craven Literacy Council
2507-F Neuse Blvd.
New Bern, NC 28562
252-637-8079, Cell: 252-671-5072
www.cravenliteracy.org

ProLiteracy

About ProLiteracy and New Readers Press

ProLiteracy believes every adult has the right to literacy. ProLiteracy, the largest adult literacy and basic education membership organization in the nation, is committed to creating a world in which all adults are literate. It works with adult new readers and learners and with local and national organizations to help adults gain the reading, writing, math, computer, and English skills they need to be successful. ProLiteracy advocates on behalf of adult learners and the programs that serve them, provides training and professional development, and publishes materials used in adult literacy and basic education instruction. ProLiteracy has 1,000 member programs in all 50 states and the District of Columbia and works with 52 nongovernmental organizations in 34 developing countries. Its publishing division, New Readers Press (NRP), has for more than 40 years provided educators with the instructional tools they need to teach adult students and older teens literacy skills for functioning in the world today. New Readers Press solicits feedback from educators during the development process. Materials are available in a variety of media, including the flagship publication, the weekly news source *News for You*, which delivers articles online with audio. Proceeds from sales of NRP materials support literacy programs in the U.S. and worldwide.

My name is Rick Adamson and I work at Craven Community College, New Bern, North Carolina, as an Academic Advisor and part time instructor. It was here I met Earl Mills in August 2007. I was the instructor for an evening College Student Success Class and Earl was a student in my class. The class was very typical for those scheduled in the evening sessions of the Fall Term, a mixture of young and old, employed and unemployed, volunteers and those being forced by parents. I have always enjoyed working with college age students because of the diversity of backgrounds that make up the class.

One of the very first assignments I have my students complete is a one to two page paper about themselves. What is so special about this first assignment is I have always asked my students to write the paper in their own hand writing instead of using a computer. I can learn much about a student just from reading their papers and analyzing their penmanship. Their grammar says a lot about their upbringing and education level. All the students are high school graduates, however, that doesn't make them educated. It only says they went to school for 12 to 14 years, not how much they learned during those years. I learned quite a bit about Earl from that first assignment. I noticed that Earl was the only student in class that submitted his paper printed instead of in cursive. His grammar was not well developed and reminded me more of an elementary student than a college student. I was soon to find out even more about Earl that was quite surprising………..he stayed after class that night and told me in private that he not only had trouble writing, he could not read very well either. Earl told me that throughout his school years, teachers had passed him just so he would move on with his class mates. Earl hid his writing and reading abilities from most everyone because he was afraid of what they may think of him. After telling me his story, I told him I would be willing to work with him as much as possible and I felt that he could be successful in the class.

This is the story I tell over and over about Earl Mills and his book report assignment in my class. The students were told to bring a book of their choosing to class so that I could approve it prior to submitting their report. Earl brought a children's book about ducks..................and.........I approved it for his report. Earl was very up front with me and told me he had never done a book report and really didn't know how to write one. I told him to read the book and just write a story about what was in the book. I was shocked when Earl turned in his report. It wasn't a story and it wasn't written like any book report I had ever read...............it was a poem. Earl had written what he was good at, and what a surprise it was to me. I hope I can locate that report so he can add it to this book. I told Earl the next week, "Earl, whatever you do in life.........don't ever quit writing your poetry!" It was probably the best report submitted out of the 20 students in the class..........oh and by the way........he made an A.

I was so honored to be asked by Earl to add just a bit to his new book. I have many years of education and have completed a Master of Arts degree in Counseling. I met many friends while serving 25 years in the United

States Marine Corps. I can honestly say, I've never met anyone with more determination and motivation to follow their life dream than Earl Mills. His dream was to be an author and a poet.................guess what............you can't tell me dreams don't come true.........because I've seen it in person.........they do!

One of the highlights of our life's journey is to witness the success of others. These experiences inspire and reinforce our own pursuits. Early on after my move to New Bern, I was fortunate to meet Earl Mills, and to subsequently be witness to his amazing journey. His story is one of persistence, commitment and focus.

Earl's eternal quest to unlock the power of the written word has inspired many – and brought a sense of admiration from all. He has proven that mountains can be climbed, that adversity can be conquered, and that commitment can be life-altering. As I've watched Earl over the years, and the reaction of those who have met him, I am in awe not only of what he has accomplished, but of the inspiration and example he has set for others.

This book, his fifth, is but another step in Earl's amazing journey from illiteracy to a master of the written word. It's been my honor and pleasure to share a small part of Earl's life. As you read this book, I encourage you to use the words in it as your own inspiration. Hop on board and join Earl in his quest for unleashing the power of words.

Bill Naumann
C E O Hatteras Yatchts
(Retired)

Earl Mills

I am thrilled that my friend Earl Mills continues to share from his life experiences through his writings and speaking, transitioning from "illiterate" adult to inspirer of all whom he encounters. I was one of those Earl "fooled" for years as we worked together, never realizing his inability to read, but always seeing the kind, caring, committed man that not only tenaciously supported his family, but his co-workers, the company for which he worked, the community and his church. When his story "broke" in the *New Bern Sun Journal*, I attempted to congratulate him as we encountered each other on the dock where we worked. In front of several other co-workers, I greeted Earl with the statement, "You are 'the man'!" Earl gave me that knowing, mischievous look that he possesses, and responded, "No, but I know 'The Man'!" Humility, service, priority! Earl "gets" what is important in life, no matter the setting, and does a masterful job of challenging us all with his words and his walk.

Don Farlow
Vice-President, Operations
Hatteras Yachts (Retired)

A

A bag of hot air means: Someone that bluffs a lot.

A ball faced lie means: When someone is telling a lie and you definitely want to get your point across that you know that their lying intentionally on purpose.

A bird bath means: To take a bath in a hand bowl or sink or to bathe quickly.

A bird in the hand is worth two in the bush means: Don't be greedy and stick with what good things you already have instead of going for something you will probably never get.

A black iron wash pot means: A three legged cast iron wash pot used for hog killings, boiling clothes, making lye soap and cooking in.

A brick house means: A woman that is shaped real fine.

A chip off the old block means: A person usually a male who behaves in the same way as his father or resembles his father.

A cockamamie ideal means: a stupid ideal, or farfetched. A cockamamie lie means: To make up a lie trying to convince someone that the story you make up is the truth.

43

A cold day in Hell means: Something you will never ever do.

And eye for an eye means: One aggressive or harmful action committed against a person is morally equal to that person committing an aggressive or harmful action towards against his or her aggressor.

A crying shame means: Something really bad has happened.

A day late and a dollar short means: You're too late.

A broken clock is right twice a day means: Because the hands are not moving the clock will be right twice a day at 6:00 A.M. and 6:00 P.M. success obtained through dumb luck.

A dead cat on the line means: To mislead or hold back information, something is going on and you can't figure what's happening, there is something wrong that you cannot see, or figure out, but that dead cat will start to smell after awhile.

A dime a dozen means: Something so common that its value is little or nothing.

A dog who will take a bone will bring a bone means: If someone is coming to you telling you all kind of things and reporting to you about someone else that same person will go and talk about you the same way.

A fast nickel is better than a slow dime means: If you have a product and you can sale it quicker and cheaper and sale more of them that better than selling them slow making that slow dime.

A frog that can't croak in his own pond is a sad frog means: A person that can't be proud of what they have accomplished.

A get together means: Friends and family coming together to fellowship.

A hand that is always closed can't receive a blessing or will not receive a blessing.

A hard act to follow means: Someone did a good job and it will be difficult for someone to do it better.

A hard head makes a soft behind part / behind means: That a person that does not listen to reason is going to have a tough life, or a child that will not listen to their parent, will get a lot of whippings or beatings.

A hard nut to crack means: Something very difficult to accomplish.

A hard row to hoe means: life or task is difficult to accomplish.

A hog is gonna (going to) go out and find pigs means: She's gonna (going to) go out and have pigs.

A hole in the wall means: Night club a little place that only has one door in and one door out or a small dingy place.

A homemade slingshot means: Made with a forked tree branch and strips of bicycle or car inner tubes, and the tongue out of a worn-out pair of shoes.

A homemade yard rake means: Made out of small tree branches that are tied together.

A horse of different color means: Talking about something of another nature you're on one subject and then someone changes the subject.

A Knee slapper means: Something very funny, when someone does or say something funny.

A leopard can't change his spot's means: You cannot change who you are.

A many uh days (a lot of days) means: Something done frequently, I have done that a many uh day.

A mile down the road as the crow flies means: Measured in a straight line.

A month of Sunday's means: A very long time without seeing someone or a time perceived as long.

A naner means: A banana.

A ounce of prevention is worth a pound of cure means: it is always easier to prevent a problem than to fix a problem.

A person that chews (bacco), (tobacco) Means, A tobacco chewer.

A problem the more you stir it the more stinker it will get.

A sapsucker, you old sapsucker, yellow-bellied sapsucker means: A derogatory state, a statement use to show this pleasure.

A slap on the wrist means: A very mild punishment, to judge very lightly.

A slow boat to China means: Moving very slow, not very productive, not in a hurry.

A snake in the grass means: a dishonest person, someone that will go behind your back.

A snowball chance in hell means: The chances of that happening is slim to none.

A snowballs chance in hell means: An unlikely chance of happening, slim possibility, something that's probably not going to make it. When someone asks you for something, you would say a snowballs chance in hell of that happening.

A spitting image means: To look like someone the exact double of another person or thing.

A steady drip of water will wear a hole in a rock means: Being consistent will overcome obstacles.

A steady drip will fill a bucket means: Being consistent will overcome obstacles.

A taste of your own medicine means: When you are mistreated the same way you mistreat others.

A watched pot will not boil means: If something is getting ready to happen if you're watching it so closely it will not happen why you are watching it.

A hog is gonna (going to) go out and find pigs means, he's gonna (going to) go out and have pigs.

Ain't studdin you (studying you) means, I'm not worried about what you are doing I do not care.

A while a ago means: A short time ago or a little while ago.

A whole new ball game means: Try something different.

A wolf in sheep's clothing means: A <u>person</u> who <u>hides</u> the <u>fact</u> that they are <u>evil</u>, with a <u>pleasant</u> and <u>friendly</u> <u>appearance</u>.

Add fuel to the fire means: To make a problem worse; to say or do something that makes a bad situation worse.

Ahhh you gon get it, imma (I am going to) tell daddy on you.

Ain't (there is not) nothing cooking but the peas in the pot and they wouldn't be cooking if the water wasn't hot means: Just a saying no meaning.

Ain't (there is not) no shame in my game means: Do something and not have any regret about it.

Ain't no (there is not)

Airn' One means: Either one .

All amongst us means: In the middle of us or in a group with us.

All bent out of shape means: Very upset, irate, angry.

All dressed up and nowhere to go means: Completely ready for something that has been postponed or has failed to materialize.

All in the bag means: If something is in the bag, you are certain to get it or to achieve it.

All over but the shouting means: Though there may be more to some process, the outcome is clear.

All over you like a cheap suit means: When someone is in your face, all over you, or in your space.

All over you like flies on crape means: All in your business.

All up into it means: Someone that is really engaged in an activity, Such as giving a job you're everything.
All wrapped up means: You finish doing something and its ready for delivery.

All you are doing is fattening the frog for the snake means: When you like someone and you're doing everything for them. And she or he really likes someone else. (Ruby Dunk, Dover, N.C.)

Am going piece a way home wet you means: A part of the way home with you.

Amongst church folks means: There are some people that don't belong in the crowd.

Amongst us means: In between us or around us among us or altogether, all in one place.

Am'un gie u (I am going to give you) something to cry about means: To discipline, to beat, to whip.

An annual hog killing a family would kill several hog in the winter, neighbors would help with the killing.

As broke as Job's Turkey means: Having little or no money, goods, or other means of support.

As country as an outhouse (and outside toilet) means: You're really country, raised country, and country acting.

As crooked as a dog's hind legs means: A road is crooked or a person is real crooked doing things that they shouldn't do also means someone who is very dishonest.

As easy as sliding off a greasy log backward means: Very easy.

As fine as frogs hair means: A frog does not have hair, scarce.

As full as a tick means: You have eaten a lot and your belly is sticking out, very full of food or drink.

As good as snuff and ain't (is not) half as dusty means: Someone who dips snuff, is an old time affection for snuff tobacco that men and women stuffed in their bottom lip or tucked inside a cheek.

As happy as a fox in a hen house means: To allow someone to be, where you would be stupid to allow them to be.

As happy as a hog eating slop means: Having a wonderful or pleasant day.

As hard as a brick means: Hard as a brick.

As hard as Chinese arithmetic means: Something that's very difficult, very hard to master, having a hard time doing.

As hard as Superman's kneecap means: Very hard.

As high as a Georgia pine means: You are drunk or intoxicated.

As hungry as I don't know what means: Very hungry, have not eaten in a long time.

As ill as a hornet means: very frustrated.

As mad as a wet stating Hen means: When a hen is sitting on her eggs, she is very protective, even to the point of anger.

As mean as a junkyard dog means: Junkyard dogs have to be mean to protect the junkyard. Some owners fed their dogs gunpowder to make them meaner.

As mean as a rattlesnake means: Dangerously mean and mean all of the time.

As messed up as and cricket in a hub cap means: Very confused, befuddled, not knowing which way to go, or what to do. A quote from Richard Boyd from Riverdale, North Carolina.

As naked as a jaybird means: Not a stitch of clothes on at all, birthday suit.

As old as the hills means: Extremely old.

As plain as the nose on one's face means: Obvious, needs no explanation, right in front of you, very odious.

As poor as a church house mouse means: Very poor, haven't had any money for a long period of time, not having one sent to your name.

As poor/broke as a convict means: Not having any money.

As pretty as all get up means: As pretty as all get up the utmost conceivable degree, a very pretty Girl or lady.

As pretty as all out doors means: As pretty as all get up the utmost conceivable degree.

As quiet as a church house mouse means: Very quiet.

As quiet as a rat peeing on cotton means: Very quiet.

As rough as a corn cob means: Not Smooth, back when you used the corn cob to wipe yourself after using the outhouse.

As scarce as hen's teeth means: There isn't any of that particular thing because hens don't have teeth.

As scared as a long tail cat in a room full of rocking chairs means: Very scared.

As serious as a heart attack means: To show that you are serious, and not joking.

As skinny as a beanpole means: Very skinny.

As skinny as a racehorse means: Very thin.

As slick as eel's snot means: Something that is very slick that you can't hold onto or grasp.

As slow as a snail means: A statement used to indicate the way an old person moves, or the movement of something when it is cold.

As slow as grandma's molasses means: Grandma's molasses poured very slow in the wintertime, so when someone was moving very slow, this was a term that was used.

As snug as a bug in a rug means: That you're comfortable in the position that you are at this junction in your life like you snuggle in bed everything is nice and comfortable.

As the crow flies, means measured in a straight line.

As tight as dicks hat band means: Someone has on really tight clothes or something fits tight.

As tough as a (liedered or light wood) knot means: to indicate the toughness or how rough a person or thing was.

As useless as tits on a boar hog means: Something that has no apparent value, no worth.

At the drop of a hat means: To do something quickly, to fly off the handle.

As mad as a wet setting hen means: Extremely angry, back in the day hens would sit on eggs to hatch them, so if you bother her it made her very angry.

B

Biggum, a big one.

Butt ugly means, completely ugly, very ugly.

Bacco (tobacco) truck means: The truck that they used to pull the bacco to the barn with a trucker or a horse.

Back in the day means, 20 or 30 years ago a while back, a long time ago.

Backed into a corner means: You have no way out, you don't have any options, you have made bad decisions and now there is nothing else to do not any options left.

Backwoods means: Country, a person that acts country, talk's country, Walk's country, dresses country, just plain country.

Bam Shamalam means: You just finished something and you are proud of it!

Barefooted and pregnant means: Women should not work outside the home and should have many children during their reproductive years. Back in the day women were having children so fast they did not have time to put their shoes back on.

Barking up the wrong tree means: You are wrong, mistaken about something, falsely accusing someone.

Bath night means: On Saturday you will get in the big wash tub all the children would take turns taking a bath in the wash tub on the back porch.

Beaten and framing means: To hit over and over again franticly, out of control, to hit emotionally, to hit something hard rapidly or repeatedly.

Beating a die horse means: That you're wasting your time probably will never amount to anything.

Beating around the bush means: Get to the point stop messing around get to directly what you are trying to say, also means to be deliberately ambiguous or unclear in order to mislead or withhold information.

Beauty is but skin deep means: Each person has a different idea of what beautiful is. Beauty is only skin deep but ugly is to the bone, beauty fades away, but ugly holds its own.

Behind the eight ball means: At a disadvantage or in a bad situation, in a losing position.

Being mannish means: Messing with older boys or girls acting fast, acting older than you really are.

Better safe than sorry means: To be cautious and to take your time, it's better to take it slow than to damage something.

Big boned means: Someone that uses their bones as an excuse for being overweight. Big wash tub was also used to wash clothes in.

Biggun' means: A big one.

Birds of a feather flock together means: People of the same sort or with the same tastes and interests will be found together.

Black as the ace of spade means: An individual who skin tone was real dark or black.

Black iron wash pot means: a pot that was used in hog killing and cooking, also used to wash clothes.

Bless his heart means: A ways to show sympathy.

Bless your heart means: A different way to say thank you.

Blind as a bat means: Not able to see well, not seeing something right in front of your face.

Blind in one eye and can't see out the other means: That something is right in your face and you can't see it, you do not see obvious things.

Blood is thicker than water means: The ties that bind are stronger when it comes to family than people outside the family.

Bone dry means: Empty and dusty, extremely empty extremely or completely dry.

Boogey means: To get out and dance.

Boo-koo money means: A lot of money or wealthy.

Both -al dem (both of them) means: I want both or all two of them.

Boy you better quit cutting-up means: a child that is always doing something wrong.

Boy you done bumped your head means: Something that's not gonna happen. Normally what a parent says when a child have done something stupid.

Boy you got a head just like your daddy means, That you and your dad are similar, you look just like your daddy.

Broke busted and disgusted means: At your wit's end with a way out, no money, and not feeling good about yourself.

Buck wild means: Uncontrollable, to lose one's mind, to act real crazy.

Burning the midnight oil means: To work studiously, especially late into the night. To work by the light of an oil lamp.

Busy as a stump-tailed cow in fly time means: very busy, not enough time to get everything done.

Butt ugly means: Completely ugly, very ugly, unattractive.

By and by when the morning comes means: It's gonna (going to) be alright after a while. Things are going to get better.

By hook or crook means: To achieve something by any means necessary, I'm going to get the job done any way I can the right way or the wrong way.

By the skin of one's teeth means: To barely make it, when you have a deadline at work, and you pull it off at the last minute.

C

Cow is gonna (going to) need a tail come fly day.

Can't beat your way out of a wet paper bag means: Someone who can't fight or who gives up easily, a person with very little tenacity.

If you can't get a word in edge wise means: Someone who talks so much and so fast that you can't get a word in or butt in.

Can't kill nothing and nothing won't die means: Not being very successful at a task or a job. Things are not going away.

Can't see the nose in front of your face means: You can't see something that is obvious.

Can't put your finger on it means: When you know you know something and it won't come to mind, when something is wrong and you know it.

Can't teach and old dog new tricks means: It is difficult to make someone change the way they do something when they have been doing it the same way for a long time.

Carrying that baby like a sack of potatoes means: Just grabbing a child any kind of way not taking care in the way that you pick them up.

Cast iron tree lagged wash or cook pot means: Is a hard, relatively brittle alloy of iron and carbon that can be readily cast in a mold and contains a higher proportion of carbon than steel.

Catching crawfish and tadpole out of the ditch and put them in jars before they would turn into frogs.

Caught between a rock and a hard place means: know where to go, in a difficult situation or limited options.

Charge it to the ground and let the rain settle it.

Cheaper by the dozen means: Something that does not have much value or is very cheap.

Cheeren: not children.

Chew on this for a while means: To study a situation, to ponder.

Chicken coop means: a wooden building with poles going from one side to the other, the chickens would roost on them at night. There would be straw bins on the side, where the chickens would lay their eggs.

Children should be seen and not heard means: back in the day when adults were talking children were not allowed to be in the conversation. They would have to go to their room or go somewhere else.

Chitterlings means: Intestines the tubes that carry food from the stomach out of the body of the hog.

Chonk-it-up- hea (here) means: To throw it up here.

City Slicker means: Is a person with the sophistication and tastes or values generally not associated with urban dwellers, typically regarded as unprincipled and untrustworthy.

Clean as a whistle means: Very clean, dressed up, looking nice.

Clean as the board of health means: The Board of Health has very high standards in cleanliness. You're dressed up ready to go, very clean.

Clear as a bell means: Easily understood, very obvious.

Clodhopper means: Heavy work shoes or large shoes.

Close but no cigar means: Fall just short of a successful outcome and get nothing for your efforts.

Clubbing means: Going out to party at the club dancing and drinking having fun.

Cock toe mighty nose means, Surprised, amazement, unexpected.

Cocked slightly to the side means: Trying to be cool, having your hat tilted to the side.

Cog knows means: God knows.

Cold water soap means: Was not boiled in a wash pot like the lye soap it was made using cold water.

Come (mo) on now means: Come on here I'm ready to go, come here or come over here.

Come hell or high water means: If you say that you will do something come hell or high water, you mean that you are determined to do it despite any difficulties that there might be: Something that has to happen no matter what it takes to get it done something that has to be accomplished no matter what it takes what hours, what money, we have to do this.

Come-on means: To go with, come-on- here.

Coming all out of the woodwork's means: They were coming from everywhere, a lot of people or things coming at you all at once.

Con-find (confound) your soul means: Boy you are always doing something you getting on my last nerve, when your frustrates with someone normally a parent with a child, is a word mama used to use when she was upset it was a word used out of frustration.

Confound your soul means: Frustrated with someone, or something.

Cooking with gas means: That you're doing it right you're up to par, you're right on target, you're doing a good job and you're doing it well.

Coon means: Raccoon.

Corn cob pipe means: The corn cob after it was dried the cob that in the center they would chew out the inside and put a read in it and it was a homemade pipe that the old men used to smoke tobacco in it.

Cotto to mighty nose means: Surprised or amazed.

Could gogga mogga means: shock and dismay or extreme appreciation.

Count your blessings means: Concentrate on all the good things in your life instead of the negative ones.

Cow is gonna (going to) need his tail come fly time means: Don't be so hasty to throw away something because you might need it one day. (Zebbie Tyson Newborn Pitt and Lenoir County North Carolina)

Cow lick means: Hair standing up on one's head.

Crack of dawn means: Very early in the morning or when the sun first comes up.

Cracklings means: The crisp pieces left after the fat has been rendered from fatty pieces of meat or skin, especially of pork.

Creek slung hog chitterlings means: When you used to go down to the creek and wash the hog chitterlings out.

Croppin' (cropping) bacco (tobacco) means: Harvesting tobacco.

Crossed eyed means: Your eyes are not straight like they should be.

Cruising for a bruising means: Looking for trouble.

Cry when you need to laugh when you can

Curing bacco (tobacco) means: When you turn the heat on to turn it brown in the tobacco barn.

Curiosity killed the cat means: You do not have to know everything, being nosy, inquisitive, sometimes it will hurt you.

Cutting a shine means: Acting a fool, cutting up, being crazy.

Cutting up means: Acting crazy.

D

Dag nabit means: Frustrated.

Da-rack'der means: After a while.

Dat (that)

Dead and gone means: When someone dies.

Dead as a doornail means: Is no longer good, it has no juice left in.

Dem, dere, (them there)

Diamond in the rough means: A person who is generally of good character but lacks manners, education, or style, someone that has not come to their Full potential yet.

Did I means: You're looking for conformation for something you did.

Did-al-le, squat means: When someone asks you for something, and you tell them that you're not going to give them did-al-le squat.

Didda means: Did I do it?

Directly means: In a little while, or a couple of weeks.

Dirt poo (poor) means: The dirt you live on does not even belong to you, real poor.

Do- hicky means: Substitute name, like the terms whata-ma-call-it or thinga-ma-jig.

Do not leave any stone unturned means: Explore every possibility.

Do not let the right hand know what the left hand is doing means: Keep something's secret, don't tell everything you know.

Do unto others as you would have them do unto you means: One should treat others as one would like others to treat oneself.

Do you want to kick that hornet nest Means: Something's are best left alone.

Does a cat have a climbing gear? Means: Something you said has been

Dog and pony show means: Unable to do a task or job efficiently because of a lack of knowledge.

Dog days means: A time of the year just before the fall of the year.

Dog gone it (gone it) frustration.

Dog gone shame means: Disgusting.

Dog gone your soul means: You are upset with someone, frustration.

Don't bite the hand that feeds you means: To turn on someone that has supported you.

Dog gone your time means: You are upset with someone, frustration.

Don (done) told ju (you) means: Now you mess with me one more time don told ju leave me alone.

Don (done) went and got yourself in a hot mess means: To get in trouble.

Don't bite off more than you can chew means: You take on more responsibilities than you can manage.

Don't blieve (believe) you're lying eyes means: When you're looking at someone do something and they are telling you don't believe what you see.

Don't burn your bridges means: Don't destroy relationships or friendships or anything because you might have to come back that way you might need it again, because you might have to go back across them again.

Don't count your eggs before they hatch means: Don't count things before you actually get them in your hand or before they actually materialize don't count anything before it comes to maturity, don't believe someone unless you know for certain, don't count on something before it is in your hands.

Don't die with your glass half full means: live your life before you go away from here, live your dreams. Do some of the things that is in your heart.

Don't flip your wig means: Don't make something out of nothing.

Don't go licking around the jar if you can't cut the mustard means: Don't mess with something that you can't handle.

Don't go off half caught means: Think it through before you do it, build it, or make it.

Don't go yet we're getting ready to open up a keg of nail means: to get the party started! Don't leave yet because I guess something is getting ready to happen. I always heard my parents say this.

Don't got no means: you don't got or have any.

Don't have two nickels to rub together means: Very poor, do not have very much money.

Don't judge a book by its cover means: Got to know someone before you judge them.

Don't let any grass grow under your feet means; Keep moving don't stay still always move forward progressing.

Don't let the green grass fool you means: People think that the greener grass on the other side of the fence is better until they have to mow the grass, people always think they would be happier in a different set of circumstances.

Don't let the right hand know what the left hand is doing means: You don't need to tell everything you're doing you need to keep something's a secret or from everybody.

Don't let them catch you with your pants down means: That you're unprepared or not ready.

Don't open up a can of worms means: Don't start nothing or uncover nothing that you can't handle, a situation or circumstance that would be best left along.

Don't put all your eggs in one basket means: diversify, don't put all your trust in one person or thing, have several options.

Don't rock the boat means: Don't cause a disturbance, leave things as they are even if they aren't ideal.

Don't say another mumbling word means: A parent or a mother disciplining a child who is talking back or someone who is angry telling a person that they have said enough don't you dare say another word.

Don't take any wooden nickels means: Don't be fooled by everything you see.

Don't talk like that imam (I'm going to) wash your mouth out with lye soap means: something a parent would tell a child when they wanted them to stop saying things that they should not saying.

Don't tell everything means: you got to have something to tell Jesus, some things you should keep to yourself.

Don't throw the baby out with the bath water means: Don't be in such a hurry that you throw out the good with the bad.

Don't upset the apple cart means: When things are going ok things are running smooth don't do anything to upset what is going on correctly or working right, going smoothly.

Done went and got yo self (yourself) pregnant means: a young girl goes out and gets pregnant.

Done went and told you means: I warned you.

Don't be running in and out of this house means: Something that parents would say when children were going in and out a lot.

Don't cut your nose off to spite your face means: A needlessly self-destructive, overreaction to a problem, do not overreact in a situation or circumstance.

Don't get your panties all in a bunch means: it's not that serious, trying to stay calm, a statement that is said to someone that gets upset easily. Do not get anxious, calm down.

Don't have enough room to cuss a cat means: Confined in a small area, not much room.

Don't let the devil ride, because he will want to drive means: If you lay down with dogs you would get up with fleas, he will make things worse than they are.

Don't- Poke-me means: Don't try to make a fool out of me.

Doo instead of door.

Dough burgers means: When I was growing up there was a lot of children so my mother would put a lot of flower in the hamburger so it would stretch them to make them go a long ways.

Down and dirty means: Doing underhanded things, be in this honest.

Down and out means: Down to your last, when someone falls on that time.

Down the road a piece means: A purt-near (long) distance, a long ways down the road, down the road a bit.

Down to earth means: Simple not thinking to highly of yourself, plain old people.

Down to the Nettie gritty means: Getting down to business, the root of something, to get to the bottom of something.

Dropped the ball means: To screw up a major opportunity, that possibly comes along only once in a blue moon.

Drunk as a skunk means: Someone is intoxicated, really sloppy drunk.

Dumb as a post means: You're not very smart not the sharpest knife in the drawer.

Dusky dark means: Just before it turns dark, at the point when the sun is setting.

E

E'rry (every)body means: all of us.

Easier said than done means: At first glance, some things look easier than they really are, not simple.

Eat the fish and spit out the bones means: Take from life what is good and spit out the Junk, be cautious of what consume.

you

Eating clay dirt means: My mama would eat the red clay dirt right out of the ground.

Eating or living high on the hog means: Eating good, eating the best parts of the hog, having plenty of money or food.

Either fish or cut bait means: Work or make way for those who will.

Elbow grease means: when scrubbing or rubbing something real hard.

Even a blind hog finds an acorn now and then means: Everyone is sometime lucky.

Every closed eye isn't sleep and every goodbye isn't gone means: Things are not always what they seem. Because a person may not mention something doesn't mean they aren't aware of it.

Every dog is going to have his or her day means: Sooner or later the sunshine will shine in everyone's life. In life everyone has a good day every now and then.

Every good bye ain't (isn't) gone means: Everything is not always as it appears to be.

Every time I turn around boy you don done something what you don done now.

Every Tom, Dick, and Harry means: Your gonna (going to) tell everybody.

Every tub must set on its own bottom means: Every person must make their own way in the world, everyone at a certain point in their life must stand on their own two feet be their own person and be self-sustaining.

Every which-al way means: This way and that way.

Everything but the kitchen sink means: used to indicate that all options have been explored.

Everything is peachy means: Everything is good well and fine.

Everything that glitters ain't (isn't) gold means: That not everything that looks precious or true turns out to be so, everything that look good aint good for you.

Everything that goes around comes around means: Whatever you did wrong to someone might hurt you in the long run.

Examine every aspect of a situation.

Eyes bigger than your belly means: When you sit down to the table and see a lot of good food you fill your plate up and cannot eat it all, you won't all the food that you see.

F

Fast as grease lightning means: Very fast.

Fast tail girl means: A young girl who is kind of fast around the boys.

Fat and sassy means: In good health and spirits.

Fat chance means: Something that is probably not going to happen, a very slim chance of happening.

Fat, dumb and happy means: Pleased with life, happy with the circumstances that surround you, enjoying life.

Fever leaves means: these leaves were use to take this swelling are fever out. Marie Mills Dover, North Carolina.

Filthy rich means: Having lots of money, very rich.

Fine as win means: Something that is pleasant or pleasing, to the eyes or mind.

Fine as wine means: you look good, you aged well.

First one thing and then another means: In life when a lot of things is going wrong when a whole lot of stuff is going wrong.

Fit to be tied means: Someone that was surprised by something that they didn't know what was going to happen, they are fit to be tied.

Fitting to go means: You about to go.

Fixing to means: About to.

Flabbergasted means: confused.

Floo instead of floor.

Foot loose and fancy free means: Not a care in the world.

Foot tub means: Was the small one that you would just put your feet in and wash your feet.

For a wasp sting, means: The spit from chewing tobacco or snuff.

From pillow to past means: Homeless, moving around, no roots.

From the frying pan to the fire means: You are going from bad worse, continually doing things to make the situation worst.

Full grown means: Adult, mature, fully developed,

G

Get 'er done (get it done) means: Quit procrastinating you have been working with this long enough.

Get up before day morning means: To get up real early in the morning.

Get up before the crack of dawn means: To get up before day light.

Get your ducks in a row means: Get your story straight before you start to tell it, make sure you have everything in order.

Get-e, (get you)

Getting old aint (is not) for sissies.

Giggle box turned over means: Someone who can't stop laughing.

Girl you need enough money to get back home means: my parents always told my sisters when they went out on a date, to always have enough money to get back home. Just in case their date started to act stupid.

Give down the country means: Give someone a piece of your mind.

Give that baby some food, milk don't make no pook or number two means: A baby needs solid food, my uncle Devbro of Trenton N.C.

Go get me ah (a) switch means: When parents would make their children go and get the switch to get a whopping with. Go hog wild means: Have a good time, to act crazy.

Go on leave me alone means: Quit bothering me.

Go whole hog means: Go for it all, to put everything into something, to mortgage the farm.

God don't like ugly means: That God doesn't like you to be mean to others or laugh and joke other people.

Going around your elbow to get to your thumb means: Going around the long way you're doing alot of unnecessary stuff.

Going to bed with the chickens means: Going to bed early in the evening, back in the day you had to get a real early jump on being in the field by sun up, so you had to go to bed with the chickens.

Going to hell in a hand basket means: Something that you're doing is going wrong everything is not going as you planned.

Gone back on your raisin (raihing) means: To deny the values that were instilled in you as a child (Deny heritage New Bern North Carolina.)

Good and hungry means: Very hungry, someone who hasn't eaten in a long time.

Good googa mooga means: Somebody do something or you see something that's hard to believe.

Good time of day means: Something amazing or something unusual.

Got here quicker than it takes a minnow to swim a dipper means: very quicker, it only takes a minnow a second to swim a dipper.

Got your feathers ruffled means: Upset and pouting, someone who gets upset very easily.

Gracious sakes a live means: To see something amazing, a statement used when someone does or says something that you can't believe they would say or do.

Grandma was slow but she was old means: Someone young acting old, someone young moving very slowly.

Great Scott means: amazing sights.

H

Half handedly means: Doing something incorrectly or not doing a good job.

Haling hind part means: You going fast, to run very quickly.

Ham (have) mercy means: Have mercy used when situations don't come out like you anticipated it, when you see something shameful or somebody acting in a shameful way.

Hand over fist means: Money is continuously coming in, good things always continually happening.

Hand-me-down means: to pass down cloth to others, when we were growing up clothes would be passed down several times.

Hankie pinkie means: Messing around.

Happy as a clam means: Everything in your life seems to be going great, everything is going well.

Happy as a dead pig in the sunshine means: Doesn't grasp or worry what's going on.

Hard headed as a belie goat means: Stubborn, will not listen to reason, does not obey.

Have been to Hell and back means: a person that has been through so much that they did not think they were going to make it.

Haven not heaven

Having children like door steps means: To have children one right after the other, every year, close to gather.

He can make a way out of no way means: The Lord is a miracle worker.

He put his pants on one leg at a time the same way I do means: That we are all equal.

He so lazy he won't hit a lick at a black snake means: a statement used to indicate when someone will not work, not even in a pie Factory.

He was going to town means: he was dancing really hard, doing something beautifully he was putting his whole self into it.

He would rather climb a tree and tell a lie, then to come down and tell the truth means: Someone that's not going to tell the truth no matter what.

Hell bent means: Really to determine to do something with all your might.

Hell was paved with good intentions means: That individuals may have the intention to undertake good actions but nevertheless fail to take action, a lot of people say their gonna (going to) do something or do better and they never do.

Hen pecked means: Someone that there wife tells them what to do, a man that does not have a back bone, not the man of the house.

Henks, a ghost , to see people that have already died.

Here chick chick chick chick means: It's a call we used to make when we throw out corn and feed for the chickens to eat. The chickens were not pinned up all day, they ran free in your fields.

He's got an ace up his sleeve means: To have a secret or surprise plan or solution to a problem.

After while, bye and bye means: It will come to pass in the future.

Hey means: Hello.

Hide bind bound means: Someone that doesn't hardly sweat, they just sweat a little.

High and mighty means: To think to highly of yourself, to believe that you are untouchable.

High handed sin means: Sinning when you know that it is wrong. You knew it was wrong when you were doing it.

High hipped means: Short torso with long legs, it gives the appearance that your hips are sitting on your back.

High yellow means: A real light skin black person, almost white.

Higher than a Georgia pine means: Someone that real drunk sloppy drunk can't stand up.

Hike-it-up means: To Jack one side up, jacked up, to lift up clock side-it.

Hind part means: The back side.

Hind sight is 20/20 means: You can always see the past better than the future.

Hit the nail on head means: To get something exactly right, Judge something correctly, to be precise.

Hitting on all eight cylinders means: An engine is working perfectly, that they doing whatever they should be doing correctly, to go along smoothly.

Hockey or get off the pot means: If you not gonna (going) to do something get out of the way so I can do it.

Hoeing bacco (tobacco) means: chopping bacco.

Hog brains and eggs means: In the days when they had hog killings, they would have hog brains and eggs for breakfast for all the neighbors that gathered to help with the hog killing.

Hog heaven means: Everything is going great, wonderful, being in a position that you thought you would never be in.

Hog killing means: To provide a supply of meat for the winter, in the fall a family would fatten and kill hogs. The neighbors assisted with the killing of the animals each family who helped with the event received some of the products.   In November or early December, two to three animals from 1.25 to 1.5 years old were penned for fattening. The customary penning period was a month or five weeks. The hogs were fed twice daily—the amount per head at each feeding, was about two quart of corn which had been soaked previously overnight in a barrel. The animals were given fresh water daily and the pens kept clean. When each animal weighed from 350 to 400 pounds it was considered ready to be killed. Previous to the day set for the killing, a pit was dug in the work yard and over it was set a large vat about 7 feet long, 2.5 feed wide flaring at the top, and 30 inches deep. Early in the morning of the killing, the vat was filled with water and a fire built in the pit underneath to heat the water for scalding the hogs. For the actual killing, one of the men used a .22 gauge rife or the bunt part of an ax. The animals were shot or hit one at a time, bleed, and plunged into the vat of hot water (147 degrees) then put on a platform and scraped with iron scrapers to remove the hair. After which, they were hung on an elevated pole by a gambrel stick put through the hamstrings of the animal (the gambrel stick varied in length from 26 to 30 inches, depending on the size of the hog). After the animal was hung, the viscera were removed while the body was still warm and the body cavity thoroughly washed. The carcasses of the animals were then left suspended in the open air to cool out. When the hog killing was over it provided an ample supply of meats for the winter like bacon, hams, sausage, blood pudding, liver, hog headcheese, hog feet, hog jowls, ribs, shoulders, pig tails

Hog tied means: secure by fastening together the hands and feet (of a person) or all four feet (of an animal) cannot get out of a situation.

Hold your horses means: Be patient, delay your actions.

Holler like a stuck pig means: Someone mislead you. They deceived you. To scream loudly.

Holy Cow means: When someone is amazed at something that happens.

Holy molly means: when something goes wrong or terribly or surprisingly something went wrong something that is surprise or amazing.

Holy rollers means: Rowdy Pentecostal church people.

Home again home again home again jiggidy jig means: You're happy to be back home back from vacation.

Home-boy means: A neighbor, a person that lives nearby, a close friend.

Homemade lye soap means: We used hog fat grease and lye with the red skull and cross bones on the can and we made the soap to take a bath with or wash your hair with or whatever and it was made in the old three legged cast iron wash pot.

Honey child what are you doing over there you pretty little thing you honey child.

Hook line and sinker means: A person who will accept a statement no matter how fan tastily foolish it might seem easy to fool or mislead.

Hope God may kill me means: A way to validate that you are telling the truth.

Hot dog all the way means: With everything on it pickles, ketchup, lettuce, chili, and relish a hot dog all the way.

How y'all dewring (How are you all doing).

Hyde bound (anhidrosis) means: Can't sweat, the inability to sweat normally or hardly sweats I first heard this in the early 70s, my wife Marie is Hyde bound.

I

Imma snatch a knot in you girl or boy means, A parent or someone is upset with their child and they're going to grab them forcefully.

I could eat a horse means: Very hungry.

I ain't got no means: I do not have any.

I ain't seen you in forever means: I haven't seen you in a long time.

I ain't gonna tell you know more means: frustrated with a child, and giving him his last warning.

I am going to be up one side of you and down the other means: To show frustration, to be up in one's face, the showing of disappointment.

I bet you a dollar to a doughnut means: To be sure our confidence in a statement or situation.

I do declare means: A statement use when something happens that you did not think was going to happen.

 I don't know you from Adam means: I didn't know you or don't recognize you, someone that you have never seen before, but they think they know you.

I done told you imam (I am going to) knock you into the middle of next week means: To strike with a hard blow.

I don't need to know how a watch is made, I just need to know what time it is means: when someone is trying to explain something and they are going on and on about it. Mike Dawson New Bern, North Carolina.

I got a bone to pick with you means: Something that you say when you want to talk to someone about something they have done that has annoyed you, we need to discuss an issue.

I got a good mind to come over there and hit you upside your head means: You mean that you would like to do it, and might do it, although you probably will not.

I got an ax to grind with you means: To have a selfish reason for saying or doing something, when someone has done something to you that you done like.

I got other fish to fry means: I'm not worried about that situation I'm concentrating on this situation here.

I just happened up on it means: To find by accident by Scott cardboard bella.

I know good-in-will (good and will) boy I know good-in-will that you ant messing with nothing that blong to me (belong to me).

I lent-it means I learn that it.

I met that means: Being serious about something that you said, standing firm on your statement.

I need that like I need a hole in the head means: Something you shouldn't do are have.

I need you like a hog needs slop means: To indicate how much you care for someone, someone you think that you cannot live without.

I put my pants on the same way you do means: A statement used to let someone know that they are no better than you are.

I reckon so means: I guess so, or perhaps it's true, I guess it's ok if you go to give permission.

I saw it with my own two eyes means: I witnessed the situation myself, to stand by what you have seen.

I thump my toe means: I hurt my toe I kick my toe against something.

I will give you something to write home to mama about means: I'm gonna (going to) tear you up, whoop you, or beat you.

I wish you God speed means: Success or good fortune, to put your blessing on a situation.

I'll be a monkey's uncle means: Expressing complete surprise or disbelief, to be surprised or amazed at something.

I'll dance at your next wedding means: To show appreciation to someone who has done something for you.

I'm afraid not means: Unfortunately no.

I'm aiming to means: Something that you're getting ready to do, thinking about doing.

I'm give slam out means: I'm tired very tired, someone that has worked real hard.

I'm gonna (going to) means: I'm going to do something to you.

I'm running late means: I'm not somewhere at the time that I should be, behind schedule.

I'm sick and tired of being sick and tired means: thoroughly weary, discouraged, or bored.

Ice potato pudding (Irish potato) white potato means: When I was growing up my mother and grandmother used to make ice potato pudding's they used the same ingredients favoring milk that you would use in a sweet potato pudding, they were delicious, you could serve it hot or cold like a bread pudding.

If a bull frog had wings means: He would bomb his butt on the ground.

If it ain't (is not) one thing it's another means: In life it seems that something is always happening or going wrong.

If it ain't (is not) broke don't fix it means: Your time would be more wisely spent working on something that needed it, leave it as it is, if something is working don't fix it.

If it had been a snake it would have bit you means: Something right in front of you, that you did not see.

If Johnny jumps off the bridge are you going to jump off the bridge too means: a statement used to discourage children from doing what other children do, d'ont do what others do.

If push comes to shove means: That it can be done if the situation becomes so bad that you have to do it, sometimes you might have to do things in a manner that you would not normally do them in.

If she doesn't jump I believe I've got her means: If things don't change I can handle them, things have been going along smoothly, if they do not change everything is gonna be okay.

If the good Lord is willing and the creek don't rise means: If something doesn't change and stay the same I'm going to do something. Do what I said, some people live on the other side of the creek and if the water rises they could not get across to do what they say they might was going to do.

If the shoe fits wear it means: If these circumstances relate to you then you should go with it, if you know you did it own up to it.

If the shoe was on the other foot means: Instead of something was happening to someone else happen to you how that would make you feel.

If you can't stand the heat get out of the kitchen means: If you can't deal with the pressures and difficulties of a situation or task, you should leave others to deal with it rather than complaining.

If you don't get out of the sun boy you gone be two shades darker.

If you don't know you better ask somebody means: Don't be messing with me.

If you don't start nothing there won't be nothing means: Do not mess with me or I'm going to finish it.

If you don't think I'm leaving just count how long I'm gone.

If you give someone an inch they will take a mile means: If you give someone liberty with something, they feel that they have liberties with other thing.

If you lay down with dogs you are going to get fleas means: If you associate with bad people, you will acquire their faults. If you're doing something you're not supposed to do something bad will happen.

If you live in a glass house you shouldn't throw stones means: People should not criticize others for faults that they have themselves.

If you make your bed hard you have to lay in it means: If you do things in life to make situations difficult you have to deal with those circumstances.

If you play with a dog he will lick you in the face means: Familiarity breeds contempt.

If you play with fire you're gonna (going to) get burnt means: Don't be messing with things that's dangerous or situations that can get you in trouble.

If you talk someone up means: If you are talking about someone and they come up, they will live a long life.

If you throw a rock in a pen full of dogs the one you hit will holler means: the guilty party will say something.

I'll be a monkey's uncle means: Amazed at someone's behavior or conduct are at something that happened.

I'll swear on my mother's grave means: I'm serious, telling the truth.

I'm going to slap the taste out of your mouth means: To slap vigorously, to slap hard, to slap continuously.

Imma (I am going to) give you something to cry about means: Back when I was growing up my parents would give me a whipping after the whipping I would be sniffling trying to stop crying, they would say boy you better hush that noise Imma give you something to cry about.

Imma (I am going to) snatch a knot in you girl or boy means: A parent or someone is upset with their child and they're going to grab them forcefully.

Imma (I am going to) tear your tail up means: When a parent is really angry with a child, what they say just before they beat you.

Imma (I am going to) kill you grave yard dead means: that someone keeps bothering you and you have already warned them to leave you alone so you use the statement (I am going to) kill you grave your dead.

Imma (I am going to) put something on you that Ajax can't take off means: to beat badly.

In a coon's age means: Been a long time.

In a heartbeat means: Quickly, very fast, will you do that in a heartbeat?

In broad daylight means: To do something in the light of day, in front of God and everybody.

In front of God and everybody means: Display in broad daylight, right out in the open, so everyone can see.

In one ear and out the other means: You're not listening or containing the information that I just told you.

In or out the house means: Stay in the house or go outside.

In the dog house means: You said something or done something bad to your spouse, normally the man. This is a term that is used to indicate that you are not in good standings at the present time you are in the dog house.

In the short rows means: Almost finished with a job or task, the end is near.

Is that chew? Means: Is that you?

Is you is or is you aint my baby.

It darned on me means: Something that comes to you automatically.

It don't take on brains to be stupid, by Pappy All.

It is a dog gone shame means: When someone does something that surprises you, when someone does something to shame themselves, a shameful act.

It is a dog, eat dog world means: That people would do anything to get to the top, even step on their best friend.

It is always darkest before the dawn means: When things seem heartless in life, is normally just before things get better, in the morning it always gets darker before daybreaks.

It taint, It is not.

It will make you or break you means: Decisions that you make or things that you decide to do, life choices will make you or break you.

It's a booger bear means: It's hard or difficult.

It's a crazy frog that won't play in his own pond means: Support your own.

It's a God's plenty means: Enough of something, it is sufficient to take care of the situation.

It's all over but the shouting means: That though there may be more to some process the outcome is clear, to have little doubt about the outcome.

It's hard as Chinese arithmetic means: It is extremely difficult, harder than anticipated.

It's monked up means: It's messed up, tow up from the floo (floor) up.

It's pouring down raining means: it's raining heavily.

It's raining like a cow urinating on a flat rock means: It's raining real hard.

It's raining like cats and dogs means: It's raining heavily, a ballet washer.

It's raining so hard it's a frog stringer means: It's raining hard.

It's so quiet in here you can hear a rat pee on cotton means: It's very quiet.

It's written all over your face means: Is saying that the expression on someone's face is showing their true feelings or thoughts.

Courage
Able Devotion
Knowledge Blessed
Conquer
Inspiration

It's all over but the shouting means: When something bad is coming to an end, when something is almost over, and you are very happy about it.

It's hard but it's fair means: Mostly used back when men and women worked hard for a living, it was all they knew so they thought it was fair.

It's like trying to get blood out of a stone means: If making someone give or tell you something is like getting blood out of a stone, it is very difficult.

It's so good that it ought to be bottled means: something that is done right, something that tastes good.

J

Jacked all up means: When you half do something, or don't do it properly and leave it all messed up.

John Brown it means: When something done go wrong and something happens and it's bad, to be frustrated, an act of frustration.

Juke joint means: Night club.

Just a skip, hop, and jump away means: Just a short distance away, it won't take very long to get there.

Just as happy as a pig in sloop means: That you're happy anyhow no matter what situation you are in.

Just as happy as if I had good sense means: Very happy.

Just as sure as God made little green apple means: To signify the seriousness of a situation.

Just as sure as grits or groceries means: Used to justify a statement.

Just as sure as pig is pork means: Used to justify a statement.

Just as sure as the sun rises means: Used to justify a statement.

Just can't win for losing means: You don't think anything is going your way. Things keep going wrong.

Just keep plugging along means: keep steady moving going on about your business.

Just whistling Dixie means: when somebody makes a statement and you know it's probably not going to come through, it don't mean nothing, it's like beating a dead hose.

K

Katy bar the doo (door) or Katy bar the gate means: That disaster impends-"watch out", "get ready for trouble" or "a desperate situation is at hand". Or when someone is upset and they are about to do something about it because they are fed up, lock her down, take precaution there is trouble ahead.

Keep your cotton pickin' (picking) hands off me means: Don't touch them, to be serious about someone not bothering you.

Keep your nose out of grown folks business means: When adults were talking back in the day children were not allowed to be in the conversation.

Kinfolk, kindred means: Family.

Knee baby names: The baby born prior to the baby is considered the knee baby, when a family has children real close to gather, and they have one before the other begins to walk, the baby would be in the lap, and the knee baby would be on the knee. The title knee baby normally follows the person into adult hood. Our sister Cynthia is still known as the knee baby to this day.

Knee high to a giraffe means: so high or tall as to reach to the knees.

Knee high to a grasshopper means: Very short.

Knock kneed means: Your knees are close together not like they should be.

Knocked up means: Pregnant

Knocking along the way (a quote by Mother Harris of New Bern, North Carolina) means: Doing fair or OK.

Knot on a log means: Just sitting not doing nothing.

Laid up means: Ill, hurt, unable to work.

L

Lawdy, Lawdy, Lawdy Miss Claudie means: Frustrated.

Lazy to the bone means: lazybones.

Lead footed means: Heavy footed, used as a statement for someone that drives very fast, Lead footed on the gas paddle.

Learnt I learnt something.

Leave well enough alone means: Don't bother with the problem anymore.

Left holding the bag means: You have been put in an awkward predicament not of your own devising or the blame of punishment everyone leaves you and you take responsibility for holding the bag.

Let it all Hang out means: To hold nothing back and to dress provocatively.

Let sleeping dogs lay means: Leave something alone if it might cause trouble: If there is something bad in the past leave it alone do not stir that pot again.

Let the chips fall where they may means: Let a circumstance or situation play out, it's gone be what it's gone be.

Let your hair down means: Relax and take it easy were not in a rush just chilling.

Liedered light-a Kindling or light wood to start a fire with means: light wood is a dated pine tree that cures in two light wood.

Life is full of moments, some to remember, some to forget, and some to cherish.

Like a bull in a China shop means: Person with no tact who upsets others or upsets plans; a very clumsy person.

Like a deer caught in head lights means: Such as widely opened eyes and a transient lack of motor reactions, to be caught by surprise.

Like a dog chasing a car means: Pursuing something that you can't do anything with, trying to bite off more than you can chew.

Like a fish out of water means: to be out of one's comfort zone, unfamiliar ground, different circumstances, unknown territory.

Like a hair in a biscuit means: That tight a biscuit baked all around the hair.

Like a train wreck looking for a place to happen means: Something that's partially broken and it's just a matter of time before it is completely broken

Like falling off a log means: Easy, no effort.

Like pulling hens teeth means: A hen does not have teeth, so this is something that you probably will not accomplish, trying to get something or do something that's hard to do, trying to get a point across to someone that don't understand.

Like putting a Band-Aid on a shot gun wound means: Not addressing the true issue/ problem, doing the minimum to take care of a situation, it will only come back later.

Like trying to find a needle in a haystack means: very hard to find, something that is very difficult to locate.

Like ugly on an ape means: If they messing with you and you won't to fight them, Very homely or ugly.

Like water on a duck's back means: A duck's back repels water, when someone doesn't let things bother them, someone that doesn't worry a lot.

Like waving a red flag in front of a bull means: Something that demands attention.

White as a sheet means: Extremely pale, as if frightened .

Like white on rice means: All over you, a statement used when someone is all up in your face, or sticking to you like glue.

Lily white means: A statement used to indicate the cleanness of something, the whiteness of something, the purity of something.

Living on a shoe string means: Getting by day to day not to have much to survive on.

Lock, Stock, and Barrel means: To possess all, someone that owns all of something.

Lolly gagging around means: Messing around not serious about what you are doing, fooling around when you should be working.

Long time no see means: Someone you haven't seen in a long time and you're happy to see them.

Look what the cat done drugged in means: Someone that you haven't seen in a while comes to see you.

Looping bacco (tobacco) means: Taking the tobacco off of the tobacco truck handing it to the looper which loops it on the tobacco stick to put it in the barn to be cure.

Loose is a person that doesn't have alot of morals; means they will do anything sexually that they shouldn't or free spirited.

Lord in habm knows (Lord in heaven knows) means: Something that you don't know.

Loud enough to wake the dead means: Like real loud music at a party, a loud engine running, people hollering.

Lying like a railroad cross tire means: Lying all the time.

106

Lying like a rug means: lying all the time.

Live to fight another day means: Survive a particular experience or ordeal.

M

Make a bull dog break a logging chain means: When you see a good looking man or good looking woman or something that's amazing.

Making mud pies means: When small girls used to play they would take dirt and make mud pie and pretend they were cooking.

Mama drug me to church means: When growing up as a small child going to church was not an option you had to go.

Mama said there'd be days like this but she didn't say they would come in bunches like bananas means: when several bad things happened in a row. Mike Dawson New Bern, North Carolina.

Mama'nem house (mother and them) means: The parents' house, our parents have been dated since 1985 and 1990, and we still called their house mama'nem house.

Man he was going to town on it means: Working hard or doing something hard.

Man she got your nose so wide open you can drive a Mack truck threw it sideways means: head over hills in love.

Man the hawks is out there means: It is cold.

Man you see him he was really cutting a rug means: Out there dancing real hard.

Mash the switch means: Press the switch.

May pops means: Slick tires that may pop at any time.

Meaner than a rattle snake means: Very meaner.

Mend fences means: Settle differences.

Mercy, Mercy me means: Looking for self pity, down hearted.

Mo means: more.

Monkey see monkey do means: Following someone's example whether it is good or bad.

Moon shine liquor means: Stump hold or homemade liquor.

Mother is going to have a cow means: When someone does something they shouldn't have they know their mother is going to be upset when she sees them and or finds out.

Mouth poked out means: Mad with someone.

108

My George, I believe I've got it means: To have something under control or to understand something.

My get up and go has got up and gone means: I don't feel too energized or willing to give 100 percent.

My plate is full means: Overloaded, doing too many things, burned out.

My, my, my means: Something looks good.

N

Nag means: To fuss, or disagree.

Naked as a jaybird means: Completely naked.

Nicknames: Shag nasty and high boot.

Nig means: Just to glaze it.

Nip it in the bud means: To stop something cold.

No ifs ands and butts means: To quit messing around, to get to the point, straight forward.

No shape form or fashion means: Don't even think about it.

No way Hoza means: Something that's probably not going to happen.

Not enough room to cuss a cat means: A real tight area.

Not for love or money means: You try to get someone to do something and they won't do it not for love nor money.

Not having two dimes to rob together means: Not having any money (broke) (poor).

Not narere-one means: Not any of you.

Not the sharpest knife in the drawer means: a statement used to indicate a low IQ, you're not very smart.

Not up to snuff means: As good as is required; meeting the minimum requirements.

Not worth a hill of beans means: worthless.

Not worth diddley squat means: Worthless, no good. A ace in the hole means: Surprise when your opponent thinks he has you down and out and you have another trick up your sleeve that your opponent doesn't know about.

Now on to 50 means: Somewhere about that age, very close estimate.

Number 3 wash tubs was a big tub to get in and take a bath.

Nun-un means: None.

O

Oh don't they look just like they self- talking about at a funeral viewing the body.

Oh me oh my means,: I'm tired I just don't feel that good I don't feel up to 100%.

Okey dokey means, Ok.

Old and worn out means: Something that has been used a lot and is no longer very useful, it has been around a long time.

Old hen means: Old lady who is past their prime always in someone else's business.

Old as dirt means; Very, very old.

Older than Methuselah means: extremely old.

On a wing and a pray means: Barely making it, I just got here by the skin of my teeth.

On your way to hell in a hand basket means: Is to be rapidly deteriorating-on course for disaster.

Once in a blue moon means: Every now and then I haven't seen you in a blue moon.

One bad apple will spoil the whole bunch means: So don't be hanging around a person that's bad influence because it will make you bad.

One foot in the grave and the other one on a banana peel means: That your living on the edge or your real sick almost about to die so old that you're not gonna (going to) live long.

One good turn deserves another means: You wash my hands I'll wash yours, do unto others as you would have them do unto you.

One monkey don't stop no show means: Just because you quit doing something doesn't mean it's not going to get done.

One of the old sayings is a big family is a happy family.

Onte-see means: I do not see.

Ont-no means: I do not know.

Ought to means, I should.

Out house means: A small wooden building outdoors that was used for a toilet.

Out in the middle of nowhere means: Last, don't know where you are not around other people.

Out of sight out of mind means: Something that you can't see you have a tendency to forget it, when something is out of sight you will forget about it.

Outhouse with a Sears and Roebuck magazine for toilet paper, definition: none.

Over yonder means: Over there.

P

Pickem' up and putem' down. Means, To run very fast.

Packed in there like sardines in a can means: To be close together, real tight.

Pat and Charlie means: Is your two feet, having to walk to your destination on your two feet.

Pecan tan means: a nice and brown skin person.

Pee pee means: To urinate

People like you come a dime a dozen means: Easy to come by, next to worthless.

Petered-out means: When you have worked long and hard and you are tired.

Piddle means: Waste time, doing nothing.

Pie in the sky means: Something good is coming in the future.

Pig ear sandwich means: Is a pig ear between two pieces of bread.

Pig inners means: The intestines, the small intestines of pigs, especially when prepared as food.

Pig Skins means: To fry the skins of a hog the outer skin of a hog.

Pin toed means: Your toes are turned in.

Pitch black dark means: When its real dark outside the moon is not shinning at all.

Playing possum means: Playing dead.

Plum tuckered out means: very tired.

Plum wore out means: Something that's not any good any more.

Poo (poor) means: You don't have anything.

Posed to means: You're supposed to have something or do something.

Pot liquor means: is the water after things like collards or string beans have been cooked, I can remember one

Christmas my grandmother Dolly Mae came to spend
Christmas with us, we told her to sit down we were cooking
Christmas for her, all of my sisters and brothers were at my
house. When we finished cooking one of the things that we
had was Collards, grandmother Dolly Mae came into the
kitchen when we finished. One of my sisters was getting
ready to throw the pot liquor out from the Collards,
grandmother Dolly May said what are you doing, you're
getting ready to throw out the best part, she say give me
that pot, and she went to work, she took that pot liquor and
made some cornbread dumplings I can still remember how
good it tasted, pot liquor was also good to mash up food in
to give to small babies.

Puddle jumper means: A little small plane.

Push water means: A phrase that is used meaning gas for a
car.

Put it on the back burner means: it's not important and we
gonna (going to) take care of it later.

Put that in your pipe and smoke it means: That what I am
telling you is the truth, you can count on it.

Putt neer means almost or just about, real close.

Q

Quiet as a church house mouse means: Very quiet.

115

Quit switching your tail like dat (that) you fast hussy.

R

Rain rain go away come again another day means: Just a saying that I used to hear older people say when it was raining a lot.

Rear back means: Lean back.

Reckon means: Think or suppose so.

Red bone means: A real light skin black person boy or girl.

Red man chewing bacco (tobacco) was a brand of chewing tobacco with a Indian on the pack.

Right off the top of someone's head means: Thinking of something and not having to research having, good memory of something.

Right out of the clear blue sky means: You was trying to think of something and couldn't remember it and then right out of the clear blue sky it comes from nowhere.

Ringer type washing machine means: is a very old washing machine at the top of the machine it had a place to ring your clothes out, it looked like rolling pins, like the ones you would roll dough out with.

Rode hard and put up wet means: Someone has lived a real ruff life they look ruff and wore out for their age. If you ride a horse real hard and not brush him down afterwards he would look real bad.

Rome wasn't built in a day means: Something that you say which means that it takes a long time to do an important job.

Root hog or die means: If a hog is left alone by himself a hog will root to find food or nourishment and probably survive.

Root worker means: To put a curse on someone.

Rowdy means: To act real badly.

Run amuck means: To run a truck into a ditch or do something stupid.

Run and tell that means: A person that feels that it is necessary to tell everything that happens, and then when something happens to that person, you would use the statement "run and tell that."

Running around like a chicken with its' head cut off means: You are the author of unorganized chaos. You have a lot going on.

Running or walking means: if you don't come on right now or hurry up you going to be walking.

117

S

Sho (sure) did means that I did do it.

Shucking and jiving is a slang term for the behavior of joking and acting evasively messing around not being truthful and doing something you shouldn't be doing.

Spose (suppose) to be means believe something is probably true.

Sand Lugs means: The bottom leaves of a tobacco stalk. When we used to pull tobacco, the bottom leaves would have a lot of sand on them I guess that's how it got its name.

Saying it don't make it so means: Just because you say it doesn't make it right.

Scalawag means: A person who behaves badly but in an amusingly mischievous rather than harmful way. The term was used derisively by white Southern Democrats who opposed Reconstruction legislation.

Scarce as hen teeth means: To be very difficult or impossible to find.

Scrimping and saving means: Economize or extremely frugal.

See if I means: Go on and see if I care.

Settin (sitting) up with the dead means: Back in the 50's and 60's when someone would die they would bring the body back to the house. People would come over and the body would be on display in one of the rooms of the house.

Shady tree mechanic means: A back yard mechanic, a do-it-yourselfer, a mechanic with no license.

Shagging hind part means: Running real fast.

Shake a leg means: Get out and dance.

Shake a tail feather means: To wiggle or dance in a shameful way jokingly or indecently.

Shaped like a coca cola bottle means: Shaped real fine, a shape of a 36 -24-36

Sharp as a tact means: You're looking good.

Shate (close) close the door.

She put her foot in it means: They did a good job cooking, a statement use when the food tastes real good
.

She's a fine mama jama means: That woman looks good.

Shindig means: Dance or celebration.

Sho (sure) did means: That I did do it.

Sho (sure) is means: I agree.

Sho' Nuff means: When someone makes a statement and you agree with them, to be in agreement.

Shouting in church means: Dancing before the Lord, praising God.

Show boating means: to show off, to bring attention to oneself.

Shucking and jiving means: Is a slang term for the behavior of joking and acting evasively messing around not being truthful and doing something you shouldn't do.

Sick as a dog means: Really sick or ill.

Six in one hand half a dozen in the other means: two things that are similar in appearance, two things that add up to the same amount.

Skating on thin ice means: To be in a risky situation.

Skinny as a bean pole means: No shape.

Slam out means: Do not have any, that it's all gone you ran out.

Slicker than Eels snot means: So slick you can't hold on to it.

Slow as molasses means: In the winner time grandmothers molasses would pour very slow.

Small fry means: Term is used when speaking to a young child.

Smelling yourself means: Is slang for being conceited.

Smokehouse means: Shed with a dirt floor where port and other meats is cured, and then smoked.

Snail pace means: Moving slowly.

Snuff dipper means: Person that dipped snuff, they would put it in their front lip, snuff made from the dust of tobacco.

So broke you can't pay attention means: Very broke.

So far so good means: At this point in the situation everything is going well.

So ugly you would scare the white off rice

Soft as a baby's behind means: Very soft and smooth to the touch.

Sooner or later means: You have to pay the cost now or either further down the road.

Sowing your wild oats means: To do wild and foolish things in one's youth.

Spanking brand New means: Something that you just purchased.

Speck and span means: Very clean.

Spider means: Is a frying pan where you cook some sausage and bacon in.

Spinning your wheels means: You're backing up and not making any progress.

Spose (suppose) to be means: Believe something is probably true, something you should be doing.

Spos-to-be means: Suppose to be.

Spring chicken means: Young thing.

Stab in the dark means: You' re basically saying you tried to come up with an answer, but you don't think the odds of actually being right are very high.

Stank not stink like a smell.

Steve Harvey said, that his father used to say, don't give someone a pin to stab you with.

Still chucking along means: Not doing 100 percent, not doing great just trying to make ends meet

Sto means: Store.

Stomping grounds means: Familiar territory.

Straight as an arrow means: Coming forth worth, something without a curve in it.

Straight from the horse's mouth means: It's coming directly from the person who said it.

Straitening comb means: A device to straitening hair, heat it up in the fire on the wood stove or fire place and put a little grease on their hair and pull it through to get the kinks and knots out of black peoples hair.

Strike while the iron is hot means: Proceed with something while it's still relevant; don't wait to pursue your dreams. Struggling like a dog means: Struggling in a difficult situation.

Strut your stuff like a model walking down the run way.

Suffering like a dog means: Going through hard times.

Sugar daddy means: A young girl or lady with an old man just for his money.

Sumpin' to eat, (something to eat)

Sumtin' (something) all the time means: Something seems to be always happening when you think things are going smooth, something unexpected.

Sun don't shine on the same dog's tail all the time means: You'll get what you deserve.

Sunday go to meet clothes means: Your best clothes.

Sweet potatoes bank means: Where you would bank your sweet potatoes using one long and one short pole to make a cross dirt and pine straw to keep them from getting cold hurt or rotting so that they would stay nice and fresh.

Sweet talking thing means: Has a good line.

Switching and swaging means: Walking provocatively.

T

The Thaing Mama nem said (The Things Mother and Them Said)

Tain't means: It is not.

Take a bird bath means: A quick bath in the hand bowl.

Taking a leak, taking a wiz, or peeing.

Talking the fire out of a burn means: When someone would get burned there was certain people in the community that could talk the fire out of a burn, there was certain words that they said and it would cause the fire out. It actually happen to me when I was 12 or 13 years old a lady talk the fire out of my arm Ms. Lewis Cindy and it was blistered and she did not touch it and I actually saw the blister bust and the pus ran out of the burn. So I've seen this personally talking the fire out of the burn.

Tape Worm means: Always hungry, a worm inside your body eating all your food.

Taters, not Irish potatoes, not sweet potatoes, just taters.

Thang au ma jing means: Something that you do not know the name of.

That a crying shame means: It is a great misfortune.

That a feature in your cap means: You done something to deserve recognition you done well and you deserve honor.

That dog won't hunt means: An obviously faulty endeavor, Someone that is not worth anything or is not productive.

That is the best thing since sliced bananas means: Something works well.

That sure enough takes the cake means: to be out done.

That went right over my head means: Not to give the gift of something and understand the consequence.

That's a hard road to hoe means: When things are tough you are going to be up against some difficult situations.

125

That's a horse of a different color means: A situation or a subject that is different from what you had first thought it was.

That's all she wrote means: That something you finished completely that you're done with.

That's gonna (going to) cost you an arm and a leg means: To be very expensive.

That's like closing the barn door after the horse is out means: Doing something too late or after the fact, like keeping a young girl home after she's already pregnant.

That's nothing to write home to mama about means: That it ain't (is not) nothing to it it's just ordinary not spectacular to it nothing to write home to mama about.

That's the pot calling the kettle black means: Someone who is talking about themselves, to be very expensive.

That's the ticket means: you got it right/ you are correct.

That's the way the cookie crumbles means: That's just the way things are.

That's water under the bridge means: Something that's past there's nothing you can do about it.

That's y'alls means: That is yours.

That's like the tail wagging the dog means: Like the workers being in charge of management, like the church members being in charge of the pastor, like the children being in charge of the parents.

The acorn doesn't fall for from the tree means: To show similarity of two things, two things being a like, a son having the characteristics of his father.

The apple don't fall far from the tree means: To be just like your parents.

The bigger they are the harder they fall means: Just because someone is big or large, does not mean that they are tough.

The black sheep of the family means: An outsider or one who is different in a way which others disapprove of or find odd.

The blacker the berry the sweeter the juice means: That things improve with time and they used to say that really dark-skinned black people were sweeter.

The boogey man means: A ghost or something will frighten a child we tell children if you be bad the boogey man will get you.

The boot of a car means: The truck, the back part where you put your tire.

The chain gang means: When the prisoner used to go out beside the road and clean the ditch banks up.

The chances of that happening, is slim to none means: An optimistic way to say one has no chance at accomplishing what he/she intends to do.

The devil takes the hind most means: If you are not careful and keep on going the devil will come up behind you and take control.

The guiltiest dog barks the loudest means: The person who reacts is responsible for an offence or misdeed.

The guiltiest pig will squeal means: also means the person who reacts is responsible for an offence or misdeed.

The harder I work the be hider I get means: Your backing up and not making any progress, spinning your wheels.

They have and they have not's means: Some people have more than others, some people don't.

The last nail in the coffin means: When a lot of things have happened, and you are frustrated, then something else happened, and it just finishes you off.

The Lord won't put more on you than you can bear means: That He prepares you to withstand anything that happens to you.

The onliest (the only) one means, the only one who did it or saw it.

The pen is mightier than the sword means: That words and communication are more powerful than wars and fighting.

The proof is in the pudding means: Once you done something proving that it works the truth will reveal itself in time.

The squeakiest wheel always gets the oil/grease means: The person who talks the loudest always gets the most attention.

The straw that broke the camel's back means: You kept doing something repeatedly and someone got tired of it, the last straw a lot of things have happened.

The tail end means: The last part, do something at the end.

The whole ball of wax means: To give everything, to put everything in.

The whole nine yards means: To give your all, everything, all-In, to put everything into something.

There ain't (is not) no if ands or buts about it means: That it is correct don't even think about it being something else.

There ain't (There's not) enough hours in the day means: When you are trying to get something done and there doesn't seem like there is enough time to do it in.

There will be trouble in River city means: the consequences of something that you have done

They ain't (is not) no fool like a old fool means: when a person has become old and still acting like a young person, a old person that did not learn when they were young.

They was a God fearing man or woman means: Pious and devout.

This is for all the marbles means: We're going for everything all money in all the bets.

This is not my first rodeo means: When you know how to do something, I know how to cook a pig.

Through thick and thin means: Through good times and bad times through good weather and bad weather.

Tickled pink means: Being very happy about something, delighted.

Tighter than dick's hat band means: Very tight.

Till the cows come home means: for an indefinitely long time, normally every afternoon a farmers cows would come home every afternoon round dark to eat.

Time waits for no man means: Life goes on. Tired and frustrated

To bail out means: To leave or desert someone.

To bank on something or someone means: To put your trust in something or someone.

To bark up the wrong tree means: To have ones attention diverted to something else or to lose attention to what you're supposed to be paying attention too.

To be as slow as a snail means: Extremely slow.

To be caught between a rock and a hard place means: In a situation where there is no solution.

To be caught with your pants down means: To be completely caught by surprise, caught off guard.

To be in a jam means: I'm in a tight spot or tough situation.

To be in hog heaven means: Everything is going your way or a situation that makes you happy.

To be in one's hip pocket means: To be in a situation where you owe someone something, and they have control over you, they have bought you, they own you.

To be in the short rows means: Almost completed or finished.

To be on someone like white on rice means: to be all over someone or something.

To be up in one's face means: To be angry with, to be upset with.

To be wore slam out means: To be exhaust, as by continued strain; weary.

To beat around the bush means: Not to get to the main topic or point of a conversation.

To beat someone down means: To beat someone down so badly, that they are unable to stop themselves from stumbling around.

To beat the ban means: They were going at it to beat the ban, putting their all into it.

To beat the black off of someone means: That a child has done something really bad and they are going to get a harsh physical punishment.

To beat the devil out of someone means: To beat someone really bad.

To beat the tar out of means: To beat someone really bad.

To beat the ugly off of someone means: To beat someone badly.

To beat you within an inch of your life means: Very close to losing one's life; almost to death.

To beat your brains out means: To hit or batter someone severely.

To bet you a dollar to a donut means: You are so confident that you will bet a dollar against nothing.

To bite the bullet means: To handle or do something that you have been dreading to deal with.

To blow out of the water means: To beat someone at something extremely bad; to defeat an opponent by a landslide.

To blow to kingdom come means: To be moved from one location to another by an explosion or the next world.

To break someone from sucking eggs means: when you're doing something and something bad happens to you that were the saying.

To break the ice means: To break down the wall of indifference between people.

To bring down the house means: To call for such wild applause like at the theatre after a wonderful performance everyone is applauding and standing up.

To bury the hatch means: To settle ones difference and take up friendly relations to put your differences aside and get along.

To be caught flat footed means: To be unprepared or undecided.

To chew one out means: To tell someone off or fuss someone out.

To cook ones goose means: One is finished; one has been found out and is in trouble.

To cool ones hill means: To be kept waiting for something, to rest, stopping of work or activity.

To cry a river means: If you're heartbroken over something or you just can't get over something.

To cry over spilled milk means: To cry over something that happened and you can't control.

To do religiously means: To do routinely.

To drag through the mud means: To slander or talk about someone or dishonor someone's name.

To eat crow means: You said something and you was wrong about the statement that you made.

To eat out of a house and home means: To eat everything that someone has in the house.

To face the music means: A situation that's bad or not good in your favor you have to man up to it.

To fall off the bandwagon means: You are going along with something and you are doing well but you regress or get off your routine. Ex: Someone has stopped drinking and then they start drinking again.

To fight like cats and dogs means: Sisters and brothers fighting hard really going at it throwing everything they got into it.

To fly off the handle means: To lose ones head, to get angry, to lose one's self control in public, to get upset or angry quickly.

To get cold feet means: Some people get cold feet when they get ready to get married, to be nervous about a situation or circumstance, hesitant about doing something.

To get on one's last nerve means: To aggravate someone to the upmost.

To get on the band wagon means: To come in agreement with something someone is organizing.

To get ones goat means: To get the best of someone to tease them and humiliate them to joke them.

To get the monkey off your back means: Jinx or something has been happening and you letting it bother you.

To get the short end of the stick means: To get less than someone else, to come up short.

To get to the nitty gritty means: To get to the bottom of a situation or circumstance.

To get up before the rooster crows means: To get up before day light.

To get your foot in the door means: To get inside of something or an organization.

To give someone a piece of your mind means: To straighten someone out fuss with them tell someone off.

To go for Broke means: To invest everything, to put all in, to mortgage the bank, 100% in,

To go hog wild means: To act or do something crazy with excitement.

To go in like it had eyes means: When something fits perfectly, to fit perfectly.

To go off halfcocked means: Not to think something out before you do it not preparing first.

To go off on a rabbit trail means: To go off topic when speaking.

To go off the deep end means: That someone has lost their mind and they are doing things that do not make any sense.

To go over someone's head means, to bypass authority.

To grease someone's palm means: To pay someone under the table or pay someone off.

To have a field day with means: To joke someone badly.

To have a hissy fit means: Someone that goes off the deep end or loses control.

To have a hitch in your giddy up means: That you have a limp or your walk is not smooth or means you're not feeling well.

To have a monkey on your back means: To be weighed down with problems, some say to have bad luck, nothing is going your way.

To have a tiger by the tail means: To take on something that is more challenging than you expected, to have more than a handful.

To have enough money to burn a wet mull means: Someone that is extremely wealthy.

To have it made in the shade means: You have life real easy, or to have a good job.

To have on a short leash means: A husband is real jealous of his wife or vice versa (to keep close watch on someone)

To have one's back against the wall means: not having any options left.

To have your back against a wall means: You don't have many options left and the person has backed you in a corner with nowhere to go.

To have your hands full means: To be in a situation where you are in over your head.

To heard it through the grapevine means: An indication that a piece of information was obtained via an informal contact.

To hit a lick and a promise means: A superficial effort made without care or enthusiasm.

To hit the high shots means: to bathe only the main areas.

To jump the gun means: To start doing something before you should or before the starting time not wait for everyone else jumping before them.

To keep one eye open means: To keep a watch on something, when you think someone is asleep, but they are peeping with one eye.

To keep the ball rolling means: To continue conversation or maintain a study flow.

To keep under your hat means: To keep something a secret to keep it to yourself not to tell anyone.

To kick the bucket means: When somebody dies.

To kick the bucket names: To die, to pass a way, to deceased.

To kick the can means, When somebody dies.

To kick to the curb means: To dump someone or to leave behind.

To kill hungry means: To eat a little something to make hunger go away.

To kill someone graveyard dead means: To get frustrated with someone's conduct so much that you are willing to take drastic measures in order to regain peace.

To kiss and tell means: To tell someone's personal business.

To kiss good bye means: To lose something, and cannot find it.

To knuckle under means: To give in to someone a pressure of a situation to stop trying and give up.

To lay down the law means: To get straight, to tell one the way that it's going to be, to be firm with what you are saying.

To lay someone out means: To tell someone off, to get someone straight, to fuss someone out.

To lay your religion down means: When someone gets upset or angry, they say that they're going lay their religion down, for a moment there not going to be saved.

To leave a bad taste in your mouth means: Something you won't ever forget, something bad happened, to be done wrong more than one time.

To leave high and dry means: To leave someone in a different situation.

To let the cat out of the bag means: To tell something that you haven't have told to break a secret to tell a secret that you should have kept.

To love to death means: To love someone so much.

To make a bull dog break the logging chain means: A statement when someone sees a man or woman that is very good looking.

To make ends meet means: To make a way out of no way to pull something together.

To make heads or tails of something means: To figure something out, to get something straight, to organize a mass, to get the understanding of something.

To make ones mouth water means: To be attractive to food you like or something you desire to make your mouth water.

To mind ones p's and q's means: To be on your best behavior to be careful of what you say or do.

To mortgage the farm means: To give everything, to go for broke, to put everything in.

To muddy up means: To mess up.

To open up a can of worms means: When things are going along smoothly, someone does something to upset the plans.

To paint the town red means: To engage in a wild spree, Origin: The allusion is the kind of riotous behavior that results in red blood being spilt, to go out with a bunch of people and hang out and have fun.

To pass the buck means: To pass the responsibility on someone else something has gone bad and you're passing the blame to someone else.

To pay under the table means: To pay in cash or in some other way.

To peep someone's whole card means: To uncover a plot.

To peter out means: To get really tired after a longs days' work, not getting any sleep, worn out.

To pick up like a sack of potatoes means: To pick up without care/ to handle roughly.

To pitch a fit or throw a fit means: To get upset angrily and throw thing.

To poke out one's lips means: A statement used to show anger or disagreement.

To pull strings means: To do something to try and gain advantage or to try and make the plan feel even to try make something happen in a situation that's not going right.

To pull the wool over one's eyes means: to get over on someone by trickery or to hide something from someone.

To put all your marbles in means: To put all in, to put in all that you have.

To put on the back burner means: To forget about it for now, to put out of your mind.

To put the cart before the horse means: When you're doing something and you don't do it in the order that it should be done in your doing it backwards your putting things that you should put last first.

To put the pedal to the metal means: To press the accelerator all the way down or to the floor, to be wide open doing something.

To put through the wringer means: To give someone a difficult time; to interrogate someone thoroughly.

To put two and two together names: To figure out, to put heads and tails together, to make things add up.

To put through the wringer means: to give someone a lot of trouble, too dill someone.

To put words in one's mouth means: When you try to influence someone, to navigate someone into saying what you want them to say.

To rake someone over the coals means: To drag or carry someone over the coal to do them in to do them harm.

To ride heard and put up wet means: A horse that was road heard and put up wet without bushing it down, I always heard it referred to a woman of the world, a loose woman.

To ride the high horse means: You think you're better than someone else.

To raise cane means: To act up, to cause a disturbance, to act wild and foolish.

To rob Peter to pay Paul means: Taking money from one thing to pay another.

To row one's eyes means: When someone doesn't like something that you say, they turned their eyes back and forth.

To rub salt in ones wound means: When someone is hurting you do something to bring even more pain to them.

To ruffle ones features means: To upset someone, to make them mad to make them furious.

To run into the ground means: To overdo something to push it passed the limit.

To see the world through rose colored glasses means: With an unduly cheerful, optimistic, or favorable view of things.

To sink like a rock means: Very fast.

To sink or swim means: When your faced with life what are you going to do about it.

To slap the taste out of one's mouth means: To slap hard, to slam in anger.

To smell ones musk means: A young adult thinks that they are grown.

To smell ones upper lip means: Someone thinks they are grown or coming of age.

To spin ones wheels means: Not to be going anyway your just making motions but you're not making any progress.

To stab someone in the back means: To go behind someone back and do something to harm them.

To stand on one's head to please someone means: Willing to do anything to make it right or to please your partner or friend or someone to stand on one's head to please someone.

To stand on your head to please someone means: To suck up to someone.

To stand on your own two feet means: To be self sufficient, being able to take care of yourself.

To stand out like a fly in a bowl of milk means: To be obvious.

To stand out like a sore thumb means: Something is so obvious or sloppy that it stands out like a sore thumb.

To steal ones thunder means: When someone takes something or an idea that is yours and uses it as their own, often in a demeaning way.

To steal the grease out of a biscuit without cracking the crust means: Someone is so skillful at stealing that they would never be detected.

To stick your neck out for someone else means: To help someone that has mad a bad decision to make a wrong decision knowing that's it's a risky deal.

To stink at something means: Is to do it poor not well.

To sugarcoat means: To down play or make little of something.

To sweat bullet means: You're scared and nervous or something scares you real bad you sweat nervously.

To take a bird bath means: To take a bath in a hand bowl or sink or to bathe quickly.

To take at heart means: To take something personally to put your emotions into something.

To take for a ride means: Is to joke someone or take advantage of someone.

To take the bull by horns means: To take a difficult danger situation at the hand, saying ill handle this situation or circumstance.

To tear one tail up means: I'm going to beat you real bad.

To tell a bald faced lie means: To knowingly lie.

To throw a fit means: To act foolishly.

To throw some water up and run under it means: You're taking a quick bath because you got to go somewhere.

To tickle your fancy means: Something happens to make your day.

To tie one on means: To get drunk or sloppy drunk.

To treat like a redheaded stepchild means: To treat different than the rest of the family, to treat differently, to treat badly.

To turn the heat up means: Put pressure on somebody.

To upset the apple court means: This expression started out as upset the cart, used since Roman times to mean" cause trouble, by spoiling ones plans' or 'to disorganize something, especially established plans.'

To use a corncob for toilet paper/ back in the day means: A long time ago.

To use a paper bag for toilet paper self – explanatory.

To use the bathroom in high cotton means: The cotton is real tall and you had a good crop that year, and you can actually squat down and use the bathroom and no one could see you in the field of cotton, you are rich.

To walk a chalk line means: You must be careful don't be messing up when you get yourself in certain situations you have to walk the chalk line.

To walk on eggshells means: To be bashful/shameful/ fearful around someone or something.

To walk through hell with gasoline underwear on means: to take a chance, to be at risk, to indicate the severity of something.

To wash up means: To take a bath.

To water down means: To make light of.

To wet one's whistle means: to get drunk: To take a drink.

To whistle Dixie means: Not serious, free.

To work into the ground means: work heard.

To work like a dog means: To work someone very hard for a long time.

To work someone like a rented mule means: You don't care that much about a rented mule so you will work him harder than one of your own.

Too big for your britches means: Mostly used when a child is doing something they shouldn't. Said when a child is acting older than their age.

Too many iron in the fire means: To be doing too many things at once, you got to many things going on at one time, you're trying to multi task.

Topping and suckling tobacco means: Taking the flower part off tobacco and sucker which grows down between the leave.

Tore up from the floor up means: Drunk or very ugly, messed up.

Tote something means: to carry something.

Tow up means: Drunk.

Trotters: Pig or sheep foot.

Two heads are better than one means: If you have a problem to solve two minds are better than one.

149

Two nickel and dime someone to death means: To keep borrowing money from someone until they are broke.

Two shades darker means: You have been out in the sun too long.

Two sheets in the wind means: Someone is really drunk.

Two wear someone out means: to beat badly or to work someone hard.

U

Umpteen times means: many times.

Until you have walked a mile in my shoes means: don't judge me until you have been where I have been, and see what I have seen.

Up the creek without a paddle means: You're in a difficult situation and you don't have anything to work with, or navigate with.

Use that head for something besides a hat rack means: To think.

Useless as tits on a boar hog means: Is a person, place, event or item in which there is little or no value.

W

Wait is what broke the bridge down means: A lot of time you need to stop waiting on something and move on it. Go ahead and do it.

Wake up and smell the roses means: stop working so much…. It's time for you to wake up and smell the roses

Walk to school in the snow uphill both ways means: To explain how tough life was in the past.

Want to means: Do you want to do something.

Wart-taker means: One who removes warts by charms or incantation.

Wash board means: That you scrub the clothes on.

Wauter, (water)

Way back then means: A long time ago.

We be kin folks means: Our family is related.

We been round this mountain before means: We done this before in the past.

We go way back means: Two people who have been friends for a long time.

We have all the bases covered means: We have studied the situation and we thought of everything that could come up.

We have beaten that horse to death means: To do consistently, to get everything there is out of something or somebody.

We know better we just don't do better.

We used to put wire in the ends of our shoe to hold them together, when the sole would come apart, we would punch a hole in the ends of the shoes with an ice pick feed the wire through it and twist it to gather with a pair of wire pliers.

We will cross that bridge when we get to it means: Let's not worry about that now, to put on the back burner, to handle later.

Well I'll be a monkey's uncle means: To surprise someone about something.

Well well well, that's a mighty deep subject for such a shallow mind.

Were in this boat together means: Something in a situation it's you and I together, we're partners in this and, we have to see it to the end.

Wet behind the ears means: You don't know much about life.

What does that have to do with the price of tea in china? means: When someone is having a conversation and someone interjects and says something unrelated to the conversation.

What want kill you, will surely fatten you.

What you doing walking around here with your mouth poked out.

What's done in the dark will come to the light means: You can't hide things that you do wrong, if we slip around and do things and we think no one sees us it might take some time because what's done in the dark will come to the light.

What's good for the goose is good for the gander means: If it is good enough for one person it is good enough for another.

When a rat fights with a cat, he better know where the rat hole is means: If your opponent is bigger and stronger, you better have a way out.

When all hell breaks loose means: When things are going will and something happens to disrupt it, a big commotion.

When donkeys fly means: When someone ask you if you believe something, and you reply with when donkeys fly.

When in Rome, do as the Romans do means: When you do something because everybody around you is doing it.

When it rains it pours means: When it seems like something is always happening, something is always going wrong, one problem after another.

When it's all said and done means: It's finished and complete now it's closed it shouldn't be anything else.

When it's raining and the sun is shining the devil is beating his wife. If you stick a pen in the ground they say you can hear him beating his wife.

When pigs fly means: When someone doesn't believe something is gonna (going to) happen it can't happen or it can't be done.

When you wrestle with a pig you get dirty, the pig gets happy means: if you lower your standards, the other person has the upper hand.

Where you born in a barn means: someone who never closes the door.

White lighting liquor means: moonshine.

Whiter than snow means: Really white.

Who dat? Means: Who is that?

Will you bring me sumthing (something) back from the sto (store).

Willy Dilly means: Carefree.

Woe (who) your feet don't fit no limb means: When you ask someone a question and they reply "who" You say you are not and owl, you comeback with this saying.

Woop sided mean: Something is crooked or cocked to the side.

Working roots on somebody means: Putting a spell on someone.

Worry wart means: One who is annoying.

Worth its weight in gold means: Something that is very valuable, something that is very rare, something sentimental.

Wrechit means: Bad, nasty, ungodly.

Wuz, (was)

Y

Ya'll or y'all means: Can be spelled both ways, you all, two or more people.

Ya'll play pretty means: Behave yourself and get along.

Yes sir re bob means: I agree with you or that's what happened.

Yon means: Not mine it's yours.

You ain't (do not have) got sense enough to get out of the rain means: Someone that does not use logic.

You ain't worth nothing coming or going, riding or walking, eating or sleeping.

You ain't got sense God gave a Billy goat means: When someone is doing something real stupid.

You aint hitting on two cent means: You're not doing anything and you're not worth anything.

You aint worth a plug nickel means: You're worthless.

You aint worth the salt in your biscuit means: there is no salt in a biscuit.

You are a chip off the old block means: To be just like someone or something, to look just like your mother father, to act like your mother father.

You are a sight for sore eyes means: I haven't seen you for a long time and I'm glad to see you.

You are as stubborn as a Billy goat means: Your hard headed want do anything that anyone tells you to do.

You are butt teethed means: Your teeth are sticking out not like they should be.

You are cheaper than dirt means: You won't spend money on anything.

You are not the only fish in the sea means: There is some else for me.

You are over the hills in love with her or hem means: you have gone slam crazy about him or her.

You are the apple of my eye means: You're a special person to me.

You are the cat's meow means: Describing a good attractive woman.

You can cool bleve (belive) that means: It is the truth.

You can lead a horse to the water but you can't make him drink means: You can't make someone do something that they do not wound to do, you can try and teach someone something, but if they don't want to learn it you are wasting your time.

You can't beat that with a stick means: That's as good as it gonna get or you can't do better than that, someone did something and they are proud of it.

You can't get blood from a turnip means: If you don't have money you can't pay a bill you can't something that you don't have, you get something out of nothing.

You can't keep birds from flying over your head, but you can keep them from building a nest in it.

You can't bet that with a stick means: Something is done correctly, right, and it's going to be hard to outdo it.

You can't change not one eye-title means: You cannot change one thing about it.

You do not have to eat a whole cow to know that you are eating beef means: you don't have to keep doing something over and over again, to get the point.

You don't want me to come over there do you means: A parent is frustrated with a child and they are down to their last straw.

You don't have a lick of sense means: You are always acting silly.

You don't have a pot to pee in or a window to throw it out of means: You don't have anything to your name that you own. To show the like of ownership.

You don't have sense enough to get out of the rain means: Someone who has trouble understanding common sense.

This is said to someone of that nature when you are frustrated with them.

You don't have sense enough to pour pee out of a boot if the direction on the heel says turn it up means: Someone who can't see past the end of their own nose, you don't have sense to figure something out or work something through. When I was about eight years old My mother used this statement, I thought she was speaking of a hill like a mountain. It wasn't until I was older that I really understood the statement, you have to turn a boot upside down to see the instructions on the heel, at that point you have already poured the pee out.

You don't have the sense God gave a Billy goat means: You are not very smart.

You don't have to nickel to rub together means: you're broke.

You don't have two words to rub together means: You don't have anything to say or add to the conversation, not very talkative.

You don't know didly squat means: You don't know anything about the subject or, situation that were dealing with.

You don't miss your water until the well runs dry means: You take things for granted.

You done gone plum crazy means: Someone that is acting weird or is doing something foolish.

You don't bump your head means: Someone that is doing stupid stuff, acting out of your mind.

You don't have sense enough to get out of the rain. Means: Someone who doesn't have or use common sense.

You don't have sense God gave a Billy goat means: Not very smart, no common sense.

You don't have to eat a whole cow to know you are eating beef means: You don't have to keep doing something over and over to learn a lesson.

You drinking all that water you gona (going to) pee the bed means: Pee in the bed when you go to bed.

You got a face that only a mother could love means: your ugly.

You got me going every switch al away means: Back and forth.

You got to crawl before you can walk means: Don't start out running a hundred miles an hour start out slow then you build yourself up to 100 miles an hour.

You got yo self in a hot mess or you gon get yo self in a hot mess means: a lot of trouble unnecessary if you keep going the way you are going

You have another thing coming means: If you think that this is going to happen, you have another think coming.

You have cold feet means: Lose your nerve and become scared and afraid.

You knuckle head means: When someone has done something wrong or something they didn't supposed to do. Acting crazy you old knuckle head, strumpet.

You lie like a rug means: A rug is always lying on the floor. Somebody say that your lying like a rug means most of everything you say is a lie, you tell a lie quick.

You little clod hopper means: You are angry with or frustrated with a child.

You look like two peas in a podmeans: Very similar, hard to tell apart, like twins.

You look like you been beat with an ugly stick means: You are very ugly.

You look like you have been drug through a knot hold backwards means: To indicate how bad something or someone looks. (Tommy Ormond New Bern N.C.)

You look like you have been rode hard and put up wet means: Someone looks real bad and ragged for their age.

You made your bed now you have to lay in it means: You have to deal with the action of your consequences.

You must aint seen me crazy yet means: You haven't seen me crazy.

You need that like you need a hole in the head means: Not to need something at all, something that you're not going to benefit from.

You need to sweep around your own front door first means: Judge yourself, before you judge others.

You not worth a grain of salt means: They use to trade slaves for a grain of salt and if you don't sell you wasn't worth a grain of salt.

You old fish-eyed fool means: that you are angry with someone.

You old geezer means: An old person who is kinda grumpy and does something that you don't like.

You old knuckle head means: When someone doing something they shouldn't do or something stupid, you old knuckle head.

You said a mouthful means: A statement used in agreement to another statement.

You scratch my back I'll scratch yours means: If you do something for me I'll do something for you.

You shameless hussy means: A woman who is kind of loose and does anything with anybody.

You sho bout dat (are you sure about that)

You should have been gone before you even got here means: You shouldn't have came.

You think you're a big shot means: A person of importance you think you're better than someone else.

You treat me like a red headed step child means: Is a person or group treated without the favor of birthright.

You trying to act high sidity means: And don't have anything, or high and mighty and don't have two nickels to rub together.

You walked right into that one means: Someone is playing a joke on you and you did not see it coming.

You wash my back I wash yours means: I got your back.

You wash my hands I'll wash yours means: One good turn deserves another.

163

You will mess up a one car funeral means: that everything you touch turns out wrong, things never go your way, always messing up.

You won't amount to a hill of beans means: You're not gonna do anything you're not gonna be successful you're not progressing you're not gonna amount to anything.

You won't hit a lick at a black snake means: Someone that won't work and is lazy and doesn't have any motivation.

You would lose your head if it wasn't attached to your body means: Someone is always losing their things.

You would lose your head if it wasn't attached to your body means: Someone that is always miss placing something, and cannot find it.

You would tear the devil means: Very destructive, a person that is always breaking or destroying something.

You would tear up the devil means: A very destructive person.

You wouldn't work in a pie factory means: Somebody is real lazy and their not gonna (going to) work no matter what.

You young whippersnapper means: A disrespectful and rude child.

You're a sight for sore eyes means: It's been forever since the last time I seen you.

You're an accident looking for a place to happen means: You're doing something foolish or something dangerous acting foolish and sooner or later you gonna get hurt.

You're as stubborn as a mule means: You're set in your old way.

You're just whistling Dixie means: You're not just talking or making small talk, you're saying something important, worthwhile.

You're not worth anything riding or walking means: you are worthless.

Young whippier snapper means: a very young person trying to do adult thing.

Your chances is slim to none means: That one has very little chance in succeeding, if any chance at all.

Your clothes looking right shabby they will think that you are a careless and perhaps poor person.

Your eyes are bigger than your stomach means: when you get a lot of food on your plate you think you're extremely hunger and you barely eat all the food.

165

Your eyes may shine, your teeth may grit, but none of this you should not get.

Your feet had better be hitting the doorsteps, when the sun touches the treetops means: In the country we did not have street lights, so the treetops were used to signify what time you had to be home, or you would get a whooping.

Your gonna (going to) bust hell wide open means: You are continually doing sinful/wrong things.

Your gonna catch your death of cold means: You are out in bad weather without the proper clothes on.

Your knocking on the door means: Your right upon something or close to something, you are approaching something within your grasp that you can contain.

Your mama had to tie a pork chops around your neck to get the dog to play with you.

Your too late that ship has already sailed means: When somebody is too old or past that part of that junction of their life.

Your two cents worth means: You opinion does not mean that much or doesn't matter.

You're acting like the world owes you something just because you are here means: A statement used when someone wants everything handed to them.

You're not worth nothing riding or walking coming or going means: someone that's not earning their keep, not willing to work, will not pull their part.

You've done went means: You have gotten yourself into trouble, you have done something wrong.

The Thangs
Mama Nem
Earl Mills
Foreword By: Doro Bush Koch
Said

Is there a book inside of you? Ever wanted to self publish but didn't know how? Concerned about the financial part of self publishing? Relax. Take a deep breath. We can help!

Finally! An affordable Self Publishing company for all of your Self Publishing needs. We have the right services, with the right prices with the right quality. So, what are you waiting for?

Unpack those dreams, break out that pen, your dreams of getting published may not be so far off after all!

Jasher Press & Co. is here to provide you with Consulting, Book Formatting, Cover Designs, editing services but most importantly inspiration to bring your dreams to past.

And this whole process can be done in less than 90 days! You thought about it, you talked about it but now is the time!

WWW.JASHERPRESS.COM
1-888-220-2068
CUSTOMERSERVICE@JASHERPRESS.COM